Dear Bev,
         With much love,
and happy reading.

                    Elisabeth.

9.11.2015

LOVE DIVINE

A devotional commentary
on the Song of Songs

LOVE DIVINE

A devotional commentary
on the Song of Songs

Elisabeth W. Wharton

Love Divine

First Published 2014.

Unless otherwise indicated, biblical quotations are from the Holy Bible, New International Version, Anglicized, NIV, Copyright © 1979, 1984, 2011 by Biblica, Inc.

ISBN 978-1-326-08686-2

Published by ER Press, Edinburgh.

Printed in UK by Lulu.com.

Dedication

This book is dedicated with love to the memory of my husband Philip, in grateful recognition of his godly grace and constant encouragement over the wonderful years we had together.

Contents

INTRODUCTION

This book in the centre of the Bible is to many scholars an enigma. Is it a love poem, or is it an allegory, as the King James Version of the Bible translates it? Is it a Syrian seven–day wedding ritual as proposed by some ancient scholars, or is it a Hebrew poem showing the influence of a Canaanite liturgy of the god and goddess of fertility?

This book of just eight chapters has caused much disagreement and controversy, and even today there is no agreement among scholars as to its author or interpretation. However, if we open our minds to the word of the Lord and trust in faith as we consider the words, we shall begin to see the meaning that the Song opens up for us. Our lives might never be the same again and we might find the peace that passes all understanding.

We read that the poem was written by King Solomon in the beginning of his rule; he was a wise and fair King. When God asked him which gift he would like to help him govern his country, he asked for the gift of wisdom; he did not ask for wealth, personal gain, and power, but instead for an enabling gift which would help him to rule justly.

The name, 'Solomon' means 'peaceful' or 'prince of peace', and God ordained that Solomon's reign of peace and plenty should foreshadow the reign of Him who is the true and only prince of Peace.

The book is a poem of praise and love. It is expressed in a romantic and radiant language. Is it a passionate poem telling of the love and devotion between a man and a young woman? Is it

Love Divine

even about the relationship between King Solomon and a maid? Others may prefer to read it as a study speaking of the relationship between the church, as the body of Christ on earth, and God our Father in heaven. However I have written this commentary to emphasise the relationship that we can have with the Holy Trinity, a close personal relationship with God the Father, Jesus Christ and the Holy Spirit.

When we begin to read through the verses we start to realise that even though the maid does not fully understand what a close relationship with the Lord is and what it will mean to her, she still has a feeling of unworthiness of such love. The world and her own life continually try to pull her away from making any commitment. She encounters derision from her own family, and even from some of her friends. Either they seem to her to be self righteous or they criticise her, declaring that she is out of balance and too single minded.

For us, the Lord will never force us to bend our knee, but if He knows that our deep desire is to follow Him, He will quietly draw us to Himself. The love and devotion of the Lord in His personal care for each one of us is continually awe-inspiring. His continual desire is to know us personally as the book of Genesis so clearly tells us. His desire is that He will become central in our lives, and to be first in all our relationships; Jesus died to pay the price for all our wrong doings to make this possible. He is the Creator of the whole world and each one of us, and when we honour Him, He will embellish any other relationship that we have, even one that is most dear to our hearts.

Introduction

One of the most popular hymns of love and devotion, often used in a wedding celebration speaks of the perfect love of God, and is a cry from us to receive that love.

Love divine, all loves excelling,
Joy of heaven, to earth come down,
Fix in us thy humble dwelling,
All thy faithful mercies crown.
Jesu, thou art all compassion,
Pure unbounded love thou art;
Visit us with thy salvation,
Enter every trembling heart. [1]

The last verse goes:

Finish then thy new creation:
Pure and spotless let us be:
Let us see thy great salvation perfectly restored in Thee.

We often sing these wonderful words speaking of the love of God, but I wonder how often these beautiful words are lost in the excitement of the day.

Milton said that true poetry is 'simple, sensuous and passionate'. All these descriptions could refer to the Song of Solomon. Many authors in both the Old and New Testament used allegorical descriptions and stories to help us understand the truths

---

[1] A hymn by John Wesley (1707-1788).

[2] I Corinthians 13:4-7.

Love Divine

that God was saying to His people, either through the patriarchs and prophets in the Old Testament, or Jesus and His disciples two thousand years ago. As William Wordsworth exclaimed:

Scorn not the sonnet……with this key
Shakespeare unlocked the heart.

Maybe this is what the Song wants to achieve in us: unlocking our hearts to accept Jesus as our Saviour, and to inherit His love.

The language of love is infinitely more than words and phrases. After a time words may seem repetitive and empty, when we need to express or show love in our life, but all the descriptions used in this book have a deep meaning and are still relevant and fresh today. This is clearly implied in the Song by the personal characters in the book. It is the only book in the Bible composed completely of direct and personal address by those in the book, the Beloved, the maid and the daughters of Jerusalem.

What do we mean by the word love? How do we define love? Is there a difference between human love and divine love?

What is the love between football fans and the players they support, the love between a man and a women, or child and its parents, or even the attachment between a human and a pet animal, or an animal that mates for life. Ultimately there can be no separating chasm between love divine and the love between humans.

Because of this fact in both the Old and New Testament we see that the marriage bond is a symbol of divine love. In marriage we make a commitment to one another, pledging that we will give

4

to each other all that we have, and honouring them for the rest of our life. If we are not married He will give us the love that 'passes all understanding' for Him alone. It is as we come to understand the divine love that our Lord gave for us on the cross, that our hearts exclaim the words of Isaac Watts:

Love so amazing, so Divine,
Demands my soul, my life, my all.

It is said that when Thomas Aquinas was dying, the monks who were looking after him asked Thomas to interpret the Song of Songs to them before he died. He said, 'Give me the Spirit of Bernard and I will do that'. The Spirit of St. Bernard of Clairvaux was certainly the key to the answer. He wrote 86 sermons on the first two chapters and three verses of the Song. He explains the bond of love from God in the Bible, and the wonder of His deep love for us, His people, with all the infinite meanings and cost of that love.

In perfect human love and love divine there can be no separating chasm, but so often 'self' undermines or taints human love by its own selfish desires. Nevertheless, in the Bible the marriage vows and consecration of that love speak of the commitment of our love to God, and His immeasurable love to each one of us. The Bible uses the relationship of two committed people to illustrate the relationship of Jesus and the church.

To quote again from Bernard of Clairvaux speaking on the Song of Solomon:

Love Divine

Love is not a cry from the mouth, but the gladness of the heart;

It is not the sounding of the lips, but the impulse and emotion of joy within; not a concert of words, but the wills moving in harmony.

Is the love that of which St. Bernard speaks the same as the love that Paul praises in 1 Corinthians 13?

If I speak in the tongues of men and of angels, but have not love, I am a noisy gong or clanging cymbal. And if I have prophetic powers, and understand all mysteries and all knowledge, and if I have all faith to move mountains, but have not love, I am nothing. If I give away all I have, and deliver my body to be burned, but have not love I am nothing.

Paul then gives a description of the very nature of Jesus. He was writing to the church in Corinth who had lost their faith and lived immorally. Paul wanted the Christians there to realise again the beauty of real love:

Love is patient and kind; love is not jealous or boastful; it is not arrogant or rude. Love does not insist on its own way, it is not irritable or resentful; it does not rejoice in

wrong, but rejoices in the right. Love bears all things,
hopes all things, and endures all things. [2]

Those words are a description of the perfect love of Jesus Christ.

What then is love? As Hugh T Kerr wrote:

It is shop-worn. It is like old money that has been worn
smooth. It is in Hollywood, in the newspaper, on the stage,
over the radio, in the pulpit, and it means something
different each time. It is a synonym for the passion to give,
and also for the passion to get. It is used in connection with
deeds of heroism and deeds of shame.[3]

Many people know and speak of criminals and murderers who have been shown the way to God by forgiveness and repentance, the way they have begun to know the love of God and consequently have completely turned their lives around to start a new life – just as St. Paul did.[4]

He was a leading Rabbi in the Jewish temple and was the most fanatical persecutor of Christians in the early church, but after he became a Christian he was a devoted servant of the Lord. He became a follower of Jesus and knew and experienced the love of God for himself and all mankind. For the rest of his life as a Christian he suffered persecution, imprisonment in chains, beatings

---

[2] I Corinthians 13:4-7.

[3] Hugh T Kerr. *The Challenge of Jesus.* (New York: Fleming H Revell Co., 1939), p. 189.

[4] Acts 9: 3-19.

Love Divine

and shipwrecks, and became one of the greatest saints of all time, all because he himself experienced the love of God. In some churches today he still is celebrated with a Feast day. The Feast of St Paul is not an anniversary of the death, or martyrdom, of a saint but a commemoration of a 'turning around' of one of the greatest teachers and thinkers of the Christian world.

We need to remember continually the love that Jesus has for us, and how he sees us now as forgiven human beings.

If anyone is in Christ, he is a new creation, the old has passed away, behold the new has come.[5].

Often it seems that we know this is a fact found in the Bible, but so often when we are caught up in the busy and often fraught life of today we forget: maybe we should stop and remember these words of St. Paul, and then proceed with more calm and grace.

My Utmost for His Highest is a book by Oswald Chambers that came into my hands in the late 1970s, after it had been reprinted for the 27th impression, and I still find it inspiring. Oswald Chambers was a saint in the early part of the 20th Century, and in Eugene H Peterson's words, 'Many millions of people have been deepened by his prayers and brought before God by his writings.'

In John 16 v 26, 27 we read, *At that day you shall ask in My name... For the Father Himself loves you.* Jesus is speaking to the

---

[5] So Paul reminds us in 2 Corinthians 5 v 17.

8

disciples of the days when he will not be with them and is telling them they will need to pray to God themselves.

Oswald Chambers says of these verses, 'He is saying… ask in My name… in other words you shall ask to my *nature,* to who I am. To My nature, not using 'my name' as a magic word.' He goes on, 'You will be so intimate with Me that you will be one with Me,'[6] Also Chambers points out that 'the day' is not a day that is past, or yet a day to come but a day meant for here and now.

The union is so complete and absolute. Our Lord does not mean that life will be free from external perplexities, but that just as Jesus knew the heart and mind of His Father, so by the baptism of the Holy Spirit will He lift us into the heavenly places, where He can reveal the counsels of God to us. 'That day' is a day of undisturbed relationship between God and each one of us.

Just as Jesus stood unsullied in the presence of His Father, so by the mighty work and wonder of the Holy Spirit within us, we can be lifted into that relationship. Jesus prayed 'that they may be one, even as we are one.' Those words are part of the wonderful awe-inspiring prayer that Jesus prayed in the garden of Gethsemane the night before He went to the cross. We must be aware that we can say those words so lightly and easily without reminding ourselves of the cost. Jesus when on this earth was a man who experienced all the joy and all the pain that we experience, but He was also the Son of God and sinless. During the First World War some men sweated blood with fear of going over the top of the dugouts. The Bible tells us that in the Garden of

---

[6] Oswald Chambers, *My Utmost for His Highest*, p.108.

Love Divine

Gethsemane, Jesus 'being in anguish, he prayed more earnestly, and his sweat was like great drops of blood falling to the ground.' Jesus knew the pain of the cross even before the events unfolded.

Dear Lord, I pray that with the gift of your grace, and the leading and guiding of your Holy Spirit in my life, I might attain that relationship, of being as one with you, and be ever drawn closer to your Father in heaven. Amen.

The psalmist King David is lost in wonder and praise as he sings to the Lord in praise of the creation of our own bodies.

I praise thee, for thou art fearful and wonderful.
Thou knowest me right well;
My frame was not hidden from you
when I was being made in secret,
Intricately wrought in the depths of the earth.
Thy eyes beheld my unformed substance;
in thy book were written every one of them,
the days were formed for me,
when as yet there was none of them. [7]

As we ponder and think about these words, we can only be amazed.

Referring to the phrase 'intricately wrought', I was told that in the original translation the same words were used to describe a thicket, or bush with all the twigs and small branches woven

---

[7] Psalm 138 v 14

together in a mass, and the same specific words were used to describe the burning bush, which was not consumed by fire. When God spoke to Moses from the bush, calling him to lead the people out of slavery to the Promised Land, He told him he was standing on Holy Ground.[8] He told Moses he wanted him to lead the people out of slavery to the promised land. To link those two occasions (the burning bush and sinews made in the depths of the earth) gives us a quickening of the heart, that any human being is held in the same standing as God held Moses.

To describe the nerves and blood vessels in our bodies as intricately wrought is such a good way to describe our blood and nervous systems, before we even begin to consider we are made in the image of God.

There is a story told of a communist in Russia trying to convince a Christian that there was no God. They had been talking for some time when the communist looked at his watch and declared that he must go, to which the Christian replied, 'You look at your watch and believe in it and act upon it, a fairly accurate and complicated instrument that man is pleased to have devised. How much greater and more intricate and more useful to you is the wrist upon which you wear it, and it is just a relatively small part of your body which no man, only God, could devise.'

The atheist student walked away to his appointment deep in thought.

It is always good to take comfort during a difficult time that God knows exactly what is happening to each one of us, and to

---

[8] Exodus 3 vv 3-7.

Love Divine

remember that we must stay close to Him, He knows the book of our lives.

Apart from our human body and all the infinite animal kingdom, we can also see the wonders of our creative God in the world that we live in.

We may only have to turn to think of a tiny flower, such as a periwinkle showing a brilliant spot of blue amongst the grass, or a weed that has pushed its way through the tarmac, and then compare those wonders to the great phenomenon of the Niagara Falls; the falls on the Canadian-U.S.A. border where 12,000 cubic feet of water per second are pitched over the huge precipice. This vast amount of water and the immense roar of noise, and enveloping splash and spray in the 167ft deep and 1,080ft wide chasm, made me think of the infinite majesty and power of our God who is the creator of the whole world with all its wonders, and galaxies of stars. Niagara is an unspeakable marvel. The rapids are manic waters and seem to boil in erratic fury, together with the sense of the sublime and awful wonder that they inspire. To some the Niagara Falls does not make them feel ecstatic, because it overawes them with the colossal dimensions of the spectacle, such as the mountains of frozen mist, and hundred feet long icicles in the winter. It is so awful, so great that after watching it for some time it gradually breaks into your conscious thinking that it must be the greatest most wonderful wonder in the natural world. To also realise that the thunder and ceaseless majesty of the torrents of water that rise and float and catch the reflections of the light in the sky were just the same when watched by the early Native

Americans. They too must have seen the spray and heard the thunderous noise when they were many miles away. When you stand watching the continuous fall of pounding water you begin to feel something of the awesome omniscient omnipresence power and majesty of our creator God who speaks to us in a still small voice.

Jesus so often pointed to nature as a revelation of God.

For those that have eyes to see, and ears to hear the
heavens declare the Glory of God.

We often fail to do that and begin to think that we are responsible for every wondrous thing in the world, and that creation is just a happy accident.

We need to view the world as God created it.

I have wonderful refreshing memories of the beautiful Yorkshire Dales, and so often I have echoed the words of my husband when he said 'It does my soul good.' Sometimes in Yorkshire the acres of heather were so clear and bright and full of bees, that it was as if we were in a beautiful private garden,

The beauty of nature is revealed throughout the eight chapters of the Song,

Not only are our thoughts turned to the silent deserts, flocks of sheep and goats and shepherds, beautiful rare sweet smelling spices herbs and fruits. We are reminded of the deep clefts in the rocks and our hidden safety in Jesus. The steep mountains, cedar trees, vineyards, and the little foxes bring much beauty to our minds.

Love Divine

This book reminds us of the flowing streams in Lebanon and the fruits and harvest in the deep valleys. We are reminded too of the cold winds of the North, which we may not enjoy but thank God for its purifying, cleansing work on the land, and then we can remember and relax in the thoughts of the soothing winds of the South and remember all the changes and wonders in the weather across the world. Even if every day is warm and sunny we may come across the catastrophic deluge of a monsoon. I remember in the safety of a home seeing young men and boys rushing out into the street naked in Indonesia, while a violent storm raged. They even had bars of soap with them to do the job of showering properly.

If we read the book just as a poem, our eyes are opened to the glory of God, and we will be enriched. The book will already have served a wonderful purpose.

CHAPTER ONE

As Christians we assent to be part of the one, Holy catholic and apostolic church, worshipping the one true God the Father, Jesus Christ His Son and the Holy Spirit. The identity of the faith is grounded in worship, and in the communion of love, which is the life of God in the Holy Trinity. It professes the faith uniquely revealed in the Holy Scriptures and written in the catholic creeds. It is therefore governed by the revelation of God and the apostolic faith in the early centuries of the Church.

The faith and order to which it witnesses are things to be received and to be handed on. When St. Paul, writing of the Eucharist, the central act of Christian worship, told the Christians in Corinth that he had 'handed on to them that which I also received', the word for 'handing on' in Greek is the word for 'tradition'. Change in the Christian Church can never be a simple endorsement of contemporary culture. Any new culture is not a new revelation, but has to be to be tested in the light of the revelation given by God, through the Hoy Scriptures and the life of Jesus Christ and then handed on from one generation to another.

There are estimated to be two billion Christians worldwide one quarter of whom are 'Pentecostals' or 'Evangelicals', not necessarily worshipping in the established churches the world over, but meeting in suitable halls, buildings or private homes, and so rapid is the growth that it is disturbing not only to atheists but to all other various religions. We might ask what gives it the power to challenge simultaneously both secular ideologies and traditional religious institutions? Quite simply because it appeals to the hunger for a direct personal experience of God, something that is neither nourished by the rationality of the Enlightenment nor just by religious dogma. To some, 'charismatic' sounds like a new phenomenon, a 'happy clappy sect' who raise their arms and dance around, singing new songs and speaking in tongues. The phenomenon most widely associated with a Charismatic church is the manifestation of the emotional release and sense of spiritual liberation as experienced at the time of Pentecost, which is described in the Book of Acts. Not all who worship in this new personal relationship speak in tongues. My own experience of these churches is that the Bible is studied as the word of God, and worship and prayer is foremost in the service, and there is a depth in the relationship amongst the people. The churches continually grow with many children in the Sunday school, young teenagers, families and people from all ages and walks of life.

This emphasis on direct spiritual experience is not a 'new thing'. 900 years ago in AD 1111 a man called Al-Ghazal died, a great thinker and polymath who wrote on a wide range of topics. His works exerted a tremendous influence on Jewish and Christian scholasticism. He not only anticipated in a remarkable way John Bunyan's *Pilgrim's Progress*, but also influenced St Thomas Aquinas, St Francis of Assisi and the scientist Blaise Pascal. We still today encourage believers to have a personal relationship with the Lord, a realisation that He knows everyone personally, and we have a relationship with Him that comes from deep in our heart. Al Ghazal called it a glass shattering experience, and referred to it as 'Tasting'. His great dictum was that 'Tasting is to know'. Those who taste know. He taught that tasting is a direct experience of truth, a realisation that goes beyond what he called the conventional learning of the age, the formal religious knowledge without the flavour imparted through inner perception. The connection between wisdom and direct experience is enshrined in the English word sapience from the Latin *sapere* to taste, and by extension, to discriminate, to know. Through 'tasting', man knows God or the inner essence of principles by means of direct apprehension or spiritual perception. It dwells in the depths of the soul and the inner aspect of the heart. This relationship and experience with God in no way defuses the need for continual studying and the need to sit at the feet of great scholars who have given their lives to studying the scriptures and revealing the truths of the Gospel. In fact this relationship increases in us the desire to learn and know more, and gives us the urge and delight to read and pray over the Gospels.

Jesus called this phenomenon, 'being born of the Spirit'.

For God so loved the world that He gave His one and only Son, that whoever believes in him shall not perish, but shall have eternal life.[9]

Paul said to the church in Philippi:

---

[9] John 3 v 16.

Love Divine

It is my prayer that your love may abound more and more,
with knowledge and all discernment,
* so that you may approve what is excellent, and may be*
pure and blameless for the day of Christ,
filled with the fruits of righteousness which comes through
Jesus Christ, to the glory and praise of God.

Studying *The Song of Songs* is a wonderful way to help us enter into a love relationship with God through Jesus Christ, and to begin to be overwhelmed by the love of God for each one of us and the love for mankind that Jesus portrayed on the cross.

Ch. 1 v 1: The Song of Songs, which is Solomon's...

So begins the introductory verse of this love poem right in the heart of the Bible. The fact that the Holy Spirit does not speak of Solomon in his earthly character in these chapters is an indication that God has inspired the book to speak to us not of Solomon but to look beneath the surface for the spiritual interpretation. Out of the one thousand and five songs that Solomon wrote, it is only this book of eight chapters that have found their way into the Holy Scriptures.

This is the Song that is above all other love songs because it speaks of the ineffable love and relationship that we can have with the Lord Jesus Christ and our Father in Heaven. The Bible describes Jesus in Colossians 1 v 18-20:

18

He is the Head of the body, the church; he is the beginning,
the first born from among the dead; so that in everything he
might have the supremacy.
For God was pleased to have all his fullness dwell in him,
and through him to reconcile to himself all things, whether
things on earth or things in heaven, by making peace
through his blood, shed on the cross.

It is as we stand in front of the Lord, holding our whole life on open palms before Him, thanking Him for the wonderful world and relationships that we enjoy, and trusting Him with any pain and sorrow that may befall us, so we begin our personal relationship with Him. We pray that in such times we might experience more of His love, and know and rejoice that he is with us at all times.

The maid begins the journey by declaring how she longs for a deep relationship with her Beloved.

V.2: Let Him kiss me with the kisses of His mouth-
For your love is more delightful than wine.

It is interesting that as the bride is close to and talking to the Lord in this opening verse she forgets to name the One for whom she is longing. Throughout the Song she never mentions His name but describes Him as her Beloved or 'The one whom my soul loves.' She speaks of Him as if there was no one else but Him on the whole earth.

The bride knows that He is near her but is unseen; there is not the close intimacy that she longs for. She longs for the kiss of love

Love Divine

and deep communion with her Beloved and to be able to always abide in His presence. Even at this stage in her relationship with Him she is aware that she is not worthy of this love but she is willing to give her life to Him so that He can melt and mould her to make her a worthy bride for a Heavenly Bridegroom. No one kisses us upon our mouth but the one to whom we are betrothed and the maid knows that this kiss will be the beginning of a new and deeper relationship.

We may experience a peck on the cheek and hug from a friend, or even a kiss on the hand signifying respect or friendship. Sadly it may be a kiss of Judas from someone we feel we cannot trust, but the kiss on the mouth, which the maid longs for, is the kiss of a bride and bridegroom.

The maid thinking of the love she craves to receive tries to describe it.

For your love is more delightful than wine.

Wine is a token of prosperity and of all good and beautiful things that we enjoy. The wine may exhilarate and give us strength or even hilarity, but it only strengthens for a time and may then leave us feeling even more vulnerable and rejected. The love of Christ is better than all earthly love and gives us a divine strength and desire that stays deep within our hearts.

We love because He first loved us.[10]

---

[10] 1 John 4 v 9.

20

The name of 'Christ' means the 'Anointed One'. When the Wise Men came from a far country to search for the Messiah, they brought to Him gold frankincense and myrrh. I watch a nativity play acted by gorgeous children on their best behaviour, with most of the cast preoccupied with looking for their adoring parents. Mary is always in blue, and Joseph with a woollen shawl and the inevitable crook, stands behind the crib knowing that he is the next most important player in this drama and the shepherds with their Mother's striped tea towels upon their heads, looking after a few cardboard sheep round about them wonder why they have to sit so still. The flotilla of beautiful angels led by Gabriel, sing to the baby in the crib, and then comes all the glitz and glamour with the three kings walking sedately down the centre aisle of the church to bring their gifts to the baby Jesus. Gold, incense and myrrh; the first gift they brought was gold, which symbolises the divinity and Kingship of Jesus. Then they brought to Him frankincense, a fragrant herb and an emblem of His glory, and they also brought to Him the sweet smelling but bitter herb of myrrh, a symbol of the bitterness and suffering of Jesus. The glory He has left in heaven, is also symbolised in the frankincense, a fragrant but also a seemingly insignificant herb, reminding us of His lowly life on earth, and the greatest gift of Himself to mankind. They also brought to Him the bitter herb of myrrh, found in the most difficult and often dangerous high places on the mountains not only speaking to us about the cost of His life and the fragrant free will of Jesus, who so humbly and cruelly paid the price for the our sins.

Love Divine

The gifts of the wise men were not just a last minute thought or casual whim as they were chosen, but were ordained by His Father. God is over all things, and nothing happens but that which He allows within the boundaries of free will.

Mary and Joseph would have been familiar with the many spices and gums, which were used in Jewish worship, and also used for the embalming of the dead. Just as God is over all things, and nothing happens to us but that which He allows - which in the world today some might find difficult to understand, our heavenly Father was in every part of the birth of Jesus, and every significant and wonderful happening at that time. We are reminded of the story our thoughts again are turned to our Beloved Lord and the glorious wonder, grace and atoning work of the cross.

The maid as she reflects upon His love begins to be aware of the beauty of her Beloved and for the first time and to realise how special and unique he is:

V.3: Your anointing oils are fragrant,
your name is oil poured out;
No wonder the maidens love you.

She is aware that her relationship with her Lord is not as deep as she longs it to be. She feels that she is not worthy of His love, and at the same time understands something of the tremendous powerful love that He has for mankind, and the sacrifice of His life for every human being, no matter what colour creed or nationality. She does not understand that to receive this love, in all its fullness will mean a total commitment of her life to Him, and not on her own terms. She must be willing to follow Him, desiring a righteous life according to the teaching of Jesus, and willingness within her to be guided by Him.

She desires a deep special meaningful relationship that will mean she will put all her trust in her Beloved. he wants the certainty that Paul exhorted the Christians in Rome to seek:

> *'that neither death nor life, nor angels, nor principalities, nor things present, nor things to come, nor powers, nor height, nor depth, nor anything in all creation, will be able to separate her from the love of God in Christ Jesus her beloved Lord.[11]*

These words perhaps speak a little extravagantly for today, but the meaning is just as poignant as when they were written:

I could not do without thee,
I cannot stand alone,
I have no strength or goodness.
No wisdom of my own
But thou, beloved Saviour
Art all in all to me,
And weakness will be powerful leaning hard on thee.

The maid tells us that she is beginning to understand something of the uniqueness of her Beloved.

---

[11] Romans 8 vv 38-39.

Love Divine

V.2: Your name is oil poured out.

This is such a devastating verse, but as we meditate upon it, we realise that the maid does understand something of the complete sacrifice that the Lord has made. He became as nothing, that we might have everything. She thinks of the stain, the mark that is left in the sand as their most precious commodity oil, is poured into it.

You cannot wipe the mark away, nor can you try to retrieve it, or scoop it up, as it was before. There is nothing – just a stain, a dark patch in the sand. Nothing.

The dark stain that is left denotes most spectacularly the work of the cross.

She turns and asks the maidens who are pure in heart, in whom she has seen a beginning of a new experience, a new relationship with the Lord. She asks if they can point her to a deeper love with her Beloved. It is only as the Holy Spirit reveals to us the Christ, and Jesus Christ reveals us to the Father, that our faith grows and we turn ever more towards God. As the fragrance and odour of the oil that has been poured out begins to steal over us: and we begin to immerse His life in our thoughts, then we begin to fathom a little more of His great love.

V.3: No wonder the maidens love you

Here at the end of the verse, the maid is speaking to those whom she recognises, those she knows who love the Lord. She begins to think of those who are pure in heart, who know something of the love of God.

Psalm 91 v 1:

He who dwells in the shelter of the Most High, who abides
in the shadow of the Almighty will say to the Lord,
My refuge and my strength my God in whom I trust.

The Beloved wants the maid to turn her thoughts around completely, and concentrate her mind on the protection, and the especial life she will have when she unequivocally turns towards Him and all He has for her. She must also be prepared to give her life more for others, taking her example from the words of Paul as he wrote to the Philippian church. He encouraged them to look to the welfare of others, taking the example of Jesus. He wants them to think more about Jesus, and remember the life that He gave up, to bring them into righteousness. This is the life that her Beloved wants the maid to enter.

Paul says:

Your attitude should be the same as that of Jesus Christ,
who being in very nature God, did not think equality with
God something to be grasped but made himself nothing ,
taking the very nature of a servant, being made in human
likeness.

Love Divine

And being found in appearance as a man, he humbled himself and became obedient to death- even death on a cross.[12]

The maid again reiterates her desire to be with her Beloved.

V.4: Take me away with you- let us hurry. Let the King draw me into His chambers.

When the bride is beginning to become aware of Him she is filled with a greater hunger and she cries, 'Take me with you.'

Already she has longed for the kisses of His mouth. She is aware of His fragrance and she remembers His life poured out for her. All these memories draw her desire to be closer to Him, and she is beginning to realise that she is helpless to run faster unless He draws her, unless He calls her.

My soul follows hard after Thee.
Thy right hand upholds me.

So said the Psalmist, who speaks of his desire to follow more deeply, to follow more closely the God he loved.

The Lord seems to have withdrawn from her, but she, like Jacob, will not let Him go. She clings to Him in prayer and communion, in obedience, in devotion and worship until He blesses her. It was after Jacob had fought and struggled with the

---

[12] Philippians 2 v 5-7.

Lord, that God touched Jacob's hip, and that great man walked away with a limp, a changed and humbled man of God.

Jacob was always a man of God, but he lived his life by tricking and deceiving others. God made a covenant with Jacob, and told him that his people would be as plenty as the dust upon the earth and all the people on earth would be blest through him and his offspring. God told him that He would watch over him until he had received all the promises that God had made with him. Jacob made a covenant with God. He said that if God did watch over him and feed and clothe him, and if he could return to his father's house, then the Lord would be his God, and everything that God had given him he would give back one tenth to God. The whole story speaks of Jacob's desires, and what would be the best for him. He would obtain his desires through trickery and deception. Eventually, when he was very wealthy and rich, Jacob did restore his relationship with his brother Esau. It was through wrestling with the God that he loved that he became a true righteous man, his natural strength reformed. His future life reflected the love, wisdom and righteousness of God. He thereafter always had to lean on his staff, a symbol of his new life and closer walk with his heavenly Father.

When the Lord has conveys to us the pathway He wants us to take, His desire is still to be with us in every part of our lives, He wants to be involved with us.

Sometimes if our nature is such that we find it difficult to wait until God opens up the way that we should go, we want to manoeuvre our life so we can make things happen. Our desire

Love Divine

maybe to do His will, but we are impatient for different circumstances to happen, and we may move before God's timing, and then every circumstance may not be the desire of God. In such times, we need to even more trust and stay close to Jesus. We are His hands and feet, but for great things to happen we must be wholly dependent upon Him, and He will show us the right way.

The verse reads 'Draw me, and let us make haste.' God will always draw each one of us, with a desire that He has put within us. Then we can do His will together. The danger is that by ourselves we may fall away because the pathway is steep and stony, forgetting that He will uphold us. If we turn away, so we will for a short time not experience His love in a deep way. If we trust and follow Him whatever the hardships may be, He will perfect in each one of us His likeness. It is as though when we have been through a refining fire the gold in each one of us becomes a pure and shining liquid.

Speaking of our place in heaven, Peter describes this testing so beautifully:

These have come so that your faith- of greater worth than gold, which perishes even though refined by fire- may be proved genuine and may result in praise glory and honour when Jesus Christ is revealed.[13]

---

[13] 1 Peter 1 v 7.

The desire of the maid is always to have her Beloved close to her, and she willingly follows Him.

V.4: Let the King bring me into his chambers.

It is only the King who can draw us into his chambers. We do not know what He requires from us as we enter in, but we trust the one we love. I picture these chambers as three stages of our deepening relationship with the Lord. The first chamber is referring to our Salvation. The door into this chamber is Jesus Christ. The Bible tells 'There is no other way in, for there is no other name given under heaven whereby men can be saved.'

The next chamber our Lord will lead us to is the Baptism of the Holy Spirit. No words can really express the peace and happiness as we pass through this door, and we know that we have truly been forgiven for all our past wrong doings. We may hear the still small voice of God saying 'There is now no condemnation for those who accept me.' It is the coming in of the person of the Holy Spirit, who is the Third Person of the Trinity, who really gives us peace. The Bible calls this peace, 'the peace that is beyond all understanding'. We begin to see that God did not save us only that we may be filled with joy, and have the promise of eternal life in heaven. His purpose is also so that we might be conformed to the image of His Son, and the gift of the Holy Spirit who will always lead and guide us towards that peace and our Father in heaven.

Hudson Taylor, was a man of tremendous faith and ability who travelled to China in the middle of the 19th Century to begin work as a missionary. He was concerned that the population of this vast country had never heard of Jesus as their Saviour, and their lives revolved round heathen gods. When he first left for China the journey took three months. Eventually he left the boat in Shanghai, and landed not knowing a single soul. He had no backing from a missionary society, no training as a minister in the church, and no career as a doctor, although he did attend a medical school for a few months.

He was a small slight man. He knew this call to China was from God and together with the Lord, and his life's work the China Inland Mission was set up.

He eventually had thousands of workers, from all over the world, working towards the same vision, scattered through the vast country of China, all supported by direct answer to prayer. They all had the same desire to bring the life of Christ to the unsaved. He tells us in his book, of the time when the workers first were aware of the work of the Holy Spirit in their lives, and their whole concept of prayer and ministering to the people was completely changed. He tells the story of one young woman who had been working in the interior for four years, and who knew something of the joy and the deep blessing to be found in working with the Master. She also felt oppressed by the deadly influences of heathenism, and the power of evil around her. She felt the blank despair of seeking to help others when her own soul was out of touch with Christ. She longed for the 'exchanged life' she saw in others but did not know how to attain it. She asked for prayer so that she might experience a new life with the Holy Spirit, and that

He might be part of her life just as she knew her risen glorious Lord was always with her.

She prayed and trusted the Holy Spirit to come into her life, just as she had prayed and trusted the Lord Jesus to be her Saviour. Feeling nothing, and realising nothing, she took God at His word, and then asked the Holy Spirit to confirm his promise, that it would be fulfilled. Her chief sorrow was that she found it very difficult to bring someone to a new faith in Jesus, so as it was the week before Christmas, she asked the Lord if she could see one person every day make a definite decision for Christ. More than 20 people made a decision that week, young and old, sailors and visitors and residents in Shanghai came to know the Lord through her direct ministry, or more correctly by Jesus working through her.

Another important testimony the Lord will call us to enter is the chamber of humility, which we must pass through before we can receive any of the attributes that He wants to give us, and those things that He wants us to achieve for His purpose.

As God works within us to soften our hearts, so that we might become humble with a compassionate nature, we may have to bow deeply to enter in through a low door. The pride that may have ruled in our hearts must be quenched, and so He may take us through this low door, and at that time we may feel that the whole world has turned against us, and rejected us. We may even feel downtrodden, but as we turn to Him we will always find He is already by our side waiting to encourage us, and sustain us. And

Love Divine

through this difficult time we will have found that He is willing to reveal more of Himself more intimately. Then we can rejoice that through that lowly painful experience we can say, 'Through it all I know more of Him.' It is a chamber that we must always be willing to enter.

Jesus was speaking of this change within us when He was speaking of the Kingdom of God, which He described as treasure worth giving everything that we hold, to gain. He used the analogy of a seed, as a seed with life at its heart and a tremendous power in its growth.

The kingdom of God is like a grain of mustard seed which a man took and sowed in his field, it is the smallest of all seeds, but when it has grown it is the greatest of shrubs and becomes a tree, so that the birds of the air come and make nests in its branches. [14]

Just as Jesus gave His life to bring life to the whole world, so if we want to bring His life to others, we must die to all our selfish desires and trust Him.

As the maid passes through the chambers of the King, love for Him thrills her heart and rises up within her. She no longer looks upon what He is doing as being the object of her search, she has begun to lose sight of the experiences and has begun to look and rejoice in Him alone.

---

[14] Matthew 13 vv 31-32.

There may be times when we are full of joy and gladness, and our lips are praising Him with a loud voice. We think we are glad and rejoicing in Him; when we really are rejoicing in our own surroundings, blessings, and gifts instead of rejoicing in Him alone. We are rejoicing in His gifts, instead of being glad in Him.

We may sometimes speak of His wonderful acts to encourage others, but we must rejoice and worship Him. We must also delight and rejoice in Him though His benefits and love seem to have been withdrawn; and even though His wonderful gifts seem to have ceased, and we feel as though we are in a dry barren land, where there is no water and manna falling from heaven we still must rejoice and trust in Him.

A friend explained that our trust and surety in the Lord is such that if we see Him a small distance away from us talking and laughing with others, we do not feel insecure and rejected, but rejoice for them in the delightful time that they are having with the Beloved.

We remember that He is only a breath away, and will never ever leave us or turn from us. We continually praise Him, though blessings may seem to fluctuate, and our circumstances change, at all times we need to remember that He never changes and will always remain the same yesterday, today and forever.

My prayer: 'I pray dear Lord, I will never despair or move away from you, but always remember and rejoice in you alone.' Amen.

Love Divine

Sometimes it is helpful to recite a simple poem or a few verses, and to just sit quietly, thinking of things that we know about Him, and listening to Him if He wants to speak to us. Very often we will find a verse of Scripture will come to our mind that we can meditate upon.

Sometimes it is when we stop our busy lives for a short while and begin to read and meditate upon such a passage as this:

O let me hear you speaking
In accents clear and still,
Above the storms of passion,
The murmurs of self will;
O speak to reassure me,
To hasten or control;
O speak, and make me listen,
Thou guardian of my soul.[15]

The maid begins to speak very openly, declaring how she feels about herself. We can pretend to others that everything is well within us, but we need to remember that our heavenly Father knows everything about us, both all that is good and all that is not the best. The Lord is always ready to heal and restore from anything in the past that might be holding us back from our relationship with Him. And the maid is beginning to realise that there are areas in her life, which are not beyond reproach, and she fears the opinion of others.

---

[15] From the hymn, O Jesus I Have Promised, words by John Bode, 1868.

34

V.5: I am very dark, but lovely, O daughters of Jerusalem,
dark like the tents of Kedar, like the curtains of Solomon,
do not stare at me because I am darkened by the sun.

When we have been touched by the Lord and want to draw closer to Him, we begin to realise our own unworthiness. The maid in her humility and consciousness of her wrong thoughts and attitudes to others likens herself to the blackness of the tents of Kedar. The Arabs of the desert covered their tents with goatskins, that are scorched black by the fierce sun, and she sees herself as dark and sinful as those black tents. She knows that her life is worthless without His love and help and she is beginning to realise that because of sin in her life, the only one who can redeem her is the Lord.

V.6: Do not stare at me because I am dark,
because I am darkened by the sun.

She is becoming aware that her past life has been lived for herself without any thought and consideration for others, and she remembers the many wrong thoughts and actions she has committed in her life. She may have begun to realise that we are all black by nature and it is only through the Lord and the work of His Holy Spirit that our life can be turned around and we can be changed from within.

She pleads with the 'daughters of Jerusalem' (Those who have turned to God and are walking closely with Him) not to stare at her, or judge her as the Lord begins to work in her life. She is fearful of what they might see. I wonder how many a young soul seeking the Lord might be intimidated by a self-righteous attitude in those around them?

Oswald Chambers explains that when we want to follow the Lord and live our lives according to His ways, we may feel inadequate and helpless. If we feel unworthy the Lord understands. We know we are not holy, nor are we likely to be. If Jesus Christ is a regenerator, One who can put into us His own heredity and nature of Holiness then I begin to see what He is saying when He says that 'We must be holy as He is Holy'. Redemption means that Jesus can put into any man the heredity disposition that is in Him, and all the standards that He gives us are based on His disposition. His teaching for us is to live by the life that He puts within us. The transaction on our part is agreement with God's verdict on sin, and in the cross of Jesus Christ, we need also to treasure and desire to become part of His life.

The New Testament teaching about regeneration, or a life turned around as Paul experienced, is that when a man is struck by a sense of need, God will put the Holy Spirit into his spirit, and our personal spirit will be energised by the Spirit of the Son of God. The revelation of the Bible is not only that Jesus Christ took upon Himself our fleshly sins, but that He took upon Himself the heredity of sin within each one of us, which no man can rectify himself. God made His own Son to be sin that He might make a sinner a saint. He took upon Himself the whole massed sin of the human race not out of sympathy, but by so doing He rehabilitated the whole human race. Jesus put mankind back to where God designed it to be. Anyone can enter into this union with God on the grounds of the work that the Lord has done upon the cross.

Jesus called Paul to Himself through a revelation of Himself on the road to Damascus. Many churches celebrate the Feast of the Conversion of St Paul. It is an interesting celebration, because it is not an anniversary of the death or martyrdom of a saint but a 'commemoration of a turning'. St. Luke records in the Acts of the Apostles how Saul, the strictest of Pharisees, who had sat at the feet of one of the greatest Jewish teachers was journeying to Damascus to persecute and put to death Christians, the followers of a 'New Way', which he regarded as heretical. He believed they were to be stamped out because they were leading the people of God astray. Suddenly, on the road to Damascus a blinding light from Heaven overwhelmed Saul, the blinding light that in the Jewish tradition was the 'shekinah,' the dazzling glory of God. Blinded, Paul falls to the ground and asks 'Who are you Lord?' To which the answer comes 'I am Jesus, whom you are persecuting.' This is the Jesus whose followers Saul had come to Damascus to kill. Blinded and stumbling Saul is led into Damascus. There three days later a Christian disciple, Ananias, comes to lay his hands on Saul that he may receive back his sight and be filled with the Holy Spirit. God completely turned life of Saul around, so that all the vigour and verve that he had shown as an enemy could be used for the glory of God as a Saint taking the Gospel to the Gentiles as well as the Jews. God also changed his name to Paul, reminding us

Love Divine

how He had changed the name of Abram to Abraham, as he began the new life that God had for him.

If you go to Damascus today you can visit the chapel on the traditional site of the house of Ananias, just off the ancient main street in Damascus, the street is still called 'Straight' as recorded in the Bible.

V.6: My mother's sons were angry with me,
they made me take care of the vineyards;
but my own vineyards I have neglected.

The maid's brothers were incensed against her, just as sometimes families react to a sibling who has started to go to Church or take on a new faith. If someone is challenged in his or her own life, because a friend or someone in the family turns towards God, the person outside the faith may become challenging, critical and even abusive. In this verse the maid's brothers 'made her work in their vineyards.' In other words they made her work on their own tasks, doing the hard work of a labourer, while all the time she was not accomplishing her own work.

The mother of the bride is referring to humanity, as represented by Eve; and it is the mother's sons, the human race, who have enticed, tempted, and taught her and brought her up in the ways of the world. It is a sobering thought when we think of the hundreds of Christians persecuted for their faith today. In this last century more people have lost their livelihood and been beaten, imprisoned and killed for their Christian faith than in all the previous 20 centuries.

May I quote a young teenager in Vietnam, a country where persecution has been more severe than in many countries? This young man has written:

The life of Peter encourages and challenges me to stand up after falling down. He was changed in a positive way and after that he preached the Gospel without fear. He was even ready to face persecution and false accusations. I pray that the Lord will change me every day so I can witness for Him. Besides that, I also learned that I must have clean hands and a pure heart- and I must be sensitive to the Holy Spirit and listen to His guidance.

Persecuted Christians live with the reality of imprisonment, violence and intimidation. For churches, persecution means secrecy and fear. It means being spied upon and monitored; buildings are targets, pastors are murdered and threatened. Organisations such as Open Doors help churches by providing support and training and by praying for Christians and leaders. They encourage pastors, and equip Christians with the resources they need to stand strong. Many persecuted Christians are doomed to a life of social exclusion and low paid jobs. Sometimes women find in the message of the Bible a source of freedom, encouragement and strength especially when their husbands are falsely accused, beaten and imprisoned. Children especially are the forgotten victims of persecution, denied education and often abandoned when parents are killed or are in prison. Teka was 14 years old when his father Yadeta Dinsa was brutally murdered after taking a service in his local church in Oromia State Ethiopa on the 15th of march 2010. Taka's mother was left to fend for her six children, she had to work the farmland, come to terms with her husband's death, comfort her children and attend crucial court hearings at the murder trial. Eventually Open Doors heard about Yadeta's murder, and after walking the five miles from the nearest town the organisation provided funds to purchase school supplies for all the children, equipment to build a new home, (after they were evicted for not being able to pay the rent) and support for Martha, Teka's mother.

'I thank God for the support and encouragement from the church and other believers' said Teka. 'My sisters are happy to have the same things as their friends in school and now I have many Fathers in the church.'

I was listening to a minister speaking about the appalling sadness and misery of the people in Mozambique. It was a service before the devotional 3-hr. Good Friday service.

He told of how the whole country is decimated by death and illness from Aids and HIV. In spite of some aid there are many child headed families who have to try to manage on their own. We silently prayed, feeling so guilty at not being able to do more to help. I am sure that most of us as we prepared for the service of the passions of the cross, were very conscious of the fact of sin within us.

Jesus never condoned sin, and I believe He must grieve daily for the sin and unjustness in the world. When He was confronted by sin, he always showed love, justness and mercy. The lone

Samaritan women at the well in the middle of the day, whom Jesus spoke to, as told in John Ch. 3, must have felt a deep cleansing and forgiveness for the wrong and sin her life, and no doubt the rejection which she was living every day, was still part of the pain. She must have felt so free and cleansed after she had talked with Jesus that she was able to run and tell all those who had judged her, that she was forgiven for all that she had done. John records that many believed that day because of her testimony, the whole village saw the change in her, and the new life that she had received.

No wonder some of the last words that Jesus spoke on the cross, in spite of all His agony and pain was 'Father, forgive them, for they do not know what they are doing.'

A doctor from a large psychiatric hospital in London said, 'If half of my patients here knew that they were forgiven, or at least were able to forgive others, they would not be here.'

We should always remember the words of Jesus on the cross. 'Father forgive them, for they do not understand what they are doing.'

I remember several years ago when I was in India with my husband. It was a beautiful warm sunny day (as it usually is in India!) and we were in a tiny Church, way out in the country south of Delhi. There were about twenty of us sitting on mats on the floor, in a small chapel. The missionary from New Zealand who had spent most of his life in India led us in a simple and very moving service, and we all took Holy Communion together. After the service the minister suggested that we should go up the steps

Love Divine

outside the small building so that we could have a better view of that part of the countryside from the flat roof. We could see an Indian woman in a saffron coloured sari drawing water from a well by the side of the building. She was from the 'Untouchable' caste of Indian, who could never talk or mix with other Indian people except from her own caste. These people always work in the hardest and most unfragrant places. We had experienced a little of this attitude in the house of friends with whom we were staying. We had our lunch, which was nicely served, but the person who had cooked it, a lady from this caste system had her lunch sitting on the floor, in the kitchen. The only hope and relief from this most dreadful class system is from the Christian Church and its members. This elderly lady at the side of the church was also drawing water from the well in the middle of the day, it took at least forty pulls to bring up the full bucket from the well, and then empty the water into a large pitcher which she eventually carried back to her home balancing it on her thick black hair.

We chatted to a young man and he told us that he was from a Hindu family and he knew there would be trouble when the family guessed that he had been to his Christian church that morning. Many families from Hindu or Muslim families in India are attacked and sometimes killed for change of faith to Christianity. During our time in India we came across many people who had been forsaken by their families. We also met many believing Christians, particularly from the work of the Indian Inland Mission who are achieving a tremendous work for the Lord.

Chapter 1

My prayer: 'Please Lord, with the grace and compassionate heart of yourself, help me to understand and pray for all those worldwide who suffer for your names sake, help me to picture those who are suffering and dejected. I pray Lord that you will draw each one to yourself with a special revelation from yourself that will comfort them, and sustain them in their distress.' Amen.

We all have something within us that only Jesus can fulfil, and the Maid in the Song of Solomon realises that she needs to know more, she is still thirsting after the love that only He can give.

V.7: Tell me, you whom my soul loves,
Where do you pasture your flock,
Where do you make it lie down at noon;
For why should I be like one who wanders
Beside the flock of your companions.

The maid has begun to realise that if she wants to know more about her Lord and to follow Him, she must seek out those who know Him and learn from them.

The reference to 'noon' in verse 7, not only refers to the Lord's passion at noon, but noon is the high point of perfection in the day. She is saying she wants to understand the deepest things about her Beloved, and all that is blessed and perfect. She does not want to sit under the ministry of those who are confused, or those who really are seeking to follow after men and personalities instead of being brought closer to Jesus.

The Lord answers her as He always does:

43

Love Divine

V.8: If you do not know, O fairest among women, follow in the tracks of the flock, and pasture your kids beside the shepherds tents.

There seems to be a slight word of reproach from the Lord as the maid asks this question. He seems to be saying, 'Have I been so long with you, and you still don't know where to find me? You should know from my word how to draw closer to me. Remember that I chose you, you are my fair one. You must be with the shepherds of my flock. Go to the green pastures and still waters where the shepherds feed their flocks, where there is no veil that will separate you from me.'

It is relevant too that the Lord also tells her to take her 'kids' with her, those to whom she is witnessing, and are still very young in their faith, so that they too can have the benefit from good teaching.

Sometimes when someone begins his walk with the Lord, and speaks excitely to his family and friends about this new relationship that he has begun, others also are drawn towards Jesus and hopefully begin to seek Him for themselves. Perhaps he may be criticised and spurned, but Paul tells us in Romans 8 God will use every situation for good for those who love Him.

We may feel very timid, and fearful that we might not understand enough ourselves, when we try to speak to others about our faith.

The Lord will always respond, even to a very quick prayer. Very soon after we had come to this new life with the Lord, I was thrown in at the deep end, so to speak. My sons who were then in

44

their teens had started a Bible study with some of their friends in our house. However one week neither of them were able to be there because of school commitments so they said, 'Mother will you do it?' I agreed and read through several times John Chapter 4, the story of the woman at the well. Unfortunately the young people were expecting me to talk on John Chapter 2! I read it with them, and still with my head down I prayed 'Lord please help me, I don't know why you changed the water into wine, *and* why it was such *good* wine.' I found my thoughts beginning to see that our life with the Lord now, was so much better than it was before we had made a positive decision to follow His ways. I realised that the 'new wine,' was symbolic of our new life in the Lord. When everyone had left I thought I hope that was the point that Jesus was demonstrating at the wedding in Cana. I should hate to suggest an incorrect meaning.

However a few days later I came across an article in a news paper saying that a speaker had opened a Christian conference, using the same passage in John's Gospel and with the same interpretation.

We don't have to be great theological students to understand the Scriptures, the Holy Spirit will not let us down if we ask Him for help. We may eventually want to study at a much greater depth so that we are able to speak and teach with a greater authority and knowledge of the Bible, but the Holy Spirit will always help us no matter how young we are in our faith.

It was written by 40 different writers, some of them highly distinguished doctors and lawyers, farmers and fishermen. They wrote about religion, poetry, ethics, science, philosophy and the creation of the universe. These people wrote about their thoughts and concerns and particularly about their knowledge of God. Their only contact with one another was by word of mouth. The information was collected at different times over a period of 1500 years, yet there is an incredible unity between the Old and the New Testaments, even though there was a 500 year gap between the writings.

The book is a universal message for all men. A book a child and scholar can delight in. Its simple life related principles are relevant for any country, transcending barriers of race and all cultures.

It is a book that can make bad men good inside, changing the rebel to a saint. The way to remain strong is to have fellowship with other Christians in Church or wherever we meet, and to get to know the Lord as our Saviour and best friend. The best way to do that is to read the scriptures faithfully and pray, as St. Frances said 'continually.' The maid is being taught by the leaders in the church, how to worship the Lord, and she has begun to know more about Jesus, and she herself has begun to teach those in her care.

The Lord then begins to speak words of comfort to her in the most beautiful language. He tells her of the lovely way He sees her in a particularly descriptive language in the Song which is such a joy to read. Especially if we identify ourselves as the maid, and join with her to know more of our God, we will be inwardly amazed at the love of God, and able to identify so much of our life with her.

So her Beloved begins to speak to her:

Vv.9-10: I compare you my love,
to a mare of Pharaoh's chariots.
Your cheeks are comely with ornaments,
your neck with strings of jewels.
We will make you ornaments of gold,
Studded with silver.

We see again that even when we make the first tentative turn towards the Jesus, He will always speak a word of encouragement, which maybe as a still small voice in our ear, or from His written word. In the Song the Lord begins to encourage her, He tells her that He sees His comeliness beginning to appear upon her.

It is important too, that the verse says 'We' will make your ornaments into gold and silver. When the Lord wants to do something special in our lives, He will always work together with us, and together the result will be of the very best.

I compare you my love, to a mare of Pharaoh's chariots.

Such an amazing description, and yet when we look into the words we are overwhelmed by the wonder of them. These are the words of comfort from her Beloved, and as so often when Jesus speaks to us, the phrases that He uses are nothing that we would dare to think of about ourselves.

Apparently the Jewish reference here is to Israel as its people fled before Pharaoh's chariots. Pharaoh's horses were famous for their value and beauty, as are Arab horses today. They were the swiftest and the most sure-footed. They could race over hills and down through the valleys, leaping over obstacles without either falling or stumbling. In battle they were obedient, they bore the chariots of war, and they also drew the chariots of pomp and glory for the Pharaoh.

These words must bring so much comfort to the maid. Sometimes we act and behave as though our Beloved is always looking at us in a critical way, forgetting that He knows our every thought and desire, and if our motives are right He will always comfort and encourage us.

The Lord knows that she has been struggling, and in danger of being overtaken by the world. It is because the bride has persevered to follow her Beloved, even though He has not led her along the way she would have liked, but she has been obedient and listened to His voice. How tenderly and graciously her Beloved speaks to her. He so often keeps His hand upon us to keep us faithful, so that He may say, 'Well done my good and faithful servant, enter into the joy of the Lord.'

Her Beloved then continues to speak of the jewels and ornaments that He sees about her face.

V.10: Your cheeks are comely with ornaments, your neck with strings of jewels.

As her Beloved refers to the maid's face as being framed with jewels, we remember that Eastern women enhance their beauty with strings of jewels or gold coins hanging down their cheeks, from underneath their veil. This gives their face the appearance of being framed in jewels.

It is this custom that is used here to describe the bride's face, ornamented with the jewels or attributes and grace of her Lord; for the jewels are symbolic of the comeliness and beauty of Christ. As God reveals to us the beauty of His Son, we realise the beauty of Him is His nature, which He wants to bestow on us. The likeness of Christ are the fruits of the Spirit, the love, joy, peace patience, kindness, gentleness, goodness, faithfulness and self-control, that Paul lists in Galatians 5 v 22.

These fruits are gifts of the Spirit to us from the Lord. Her Beloved sees these fruits reflected in her face, and He rejoices. We must not think that we have earned them because we are special. Yet if we have been given them and the Lord has put them on us, we shall not be aware of them. Just as we cannot look at our own face except through a mirror, so it is with the bride of Christ; she will not see her face when it is framed with these beautiful attributes of the Lord.

Some of the jewels surrounding the face of the maid are also the gifts, which God gives us to enable us to help and serve others and to use when we are ministering to others and teaching the Gospel of Christ. We can also call upon them during our everyday lives, using them to enable us to be more efficient and loving people.

These jewels, the fruits and gifts of the Sprit are listed and spoken about in a letter from Paul to the church in Corinth, a very wicked and corrupt city in these early times. The few Christians

Love Divine

would need all the wisdom and love of Christ to preach and minister to others.

Paul reminds the Christians in Corinth that we are all part of the Body of Christ on earth with Christ as the head of the Body, and we are His hands and feet listed in 1 Corinthians 12 v 28:

And God has appointed in the church first apostles, second prophets,
Third teachers, then workers of miracles, then healers, helpers, administrators, speakers in various kinds of tongues.
Are all apostles?
Are all prophets?
Are all teachers?
Do all work miracles?
Do all posses gifts of healing?
Do all speak with tongues?
Do all interpret?
But earnestly desire the higher gifts.
All these are inspired by one and the same Spirit, who apportions to all as he wills.

As we pray for these gifts, knowing that God has everything planned for us right from the beginning of our lives, we will learn to use them and be more efficient as a servant for our Saviour. As we begin to have the need of a gift God will give them as the need arises. He will confirm the gift in you, and also the mature Christians and leaders of the Church will encourage you.

50

Chapter 1

In 1994 a young man named Salavat Serikbayev in Uzbekistan became a Christian in his hometown of Muinaq, Karakalpakstan. He was just 19 years old, He was given a New Testament and became the pastor of a small group of believers. He had never read the Bible before, but every day he took one verse, explained it to the people, and this group of believers grew.

Salavat is married to Aitgul and they have five children aged between one and ten. Opposition from relatives, society and the authorities has become part of their life. He was jailed for four months in 1999 and offered freedom only if he would reject Christianity. Aitgul lost her job. Once an angry crowd surrounded their house, threatening to set it on fire.

When Salavat returned home from prison, there was no food or money in the house. As he and Aitgul prayed in desperation there was a knock at the door. Two men explained they were driving by and had felt that they had to come to the house. They handed over a parcel and left. Salavat went outside to see them go, but there was no sign of them, or a car. The parcel contained enough money to keep the family for one month. When Salavat told his three-year-old daughter what had happened she said, 'Can I call your God my God?'

Many Christians have heard of similar experiences, and have also experienced similar miracles in their lives.

A prayer: 'Please Lord, we pray for health and strength and endurance for Salavat, and his family. We also pray for Aitgul and her children in these very difficult times. We pray for all those who

Love Divine

are suffering, and in pain at this time, that even in their affliction and sorrow they will feel and know your presence with them.'

Amen.

There are ornaments of gold and silver which the maid's Beloved sees adorning her face, they remind us of the perfection and deity of God that is beginning to shine from her. The silver reminds us that this metal is heated and hammered to bring it into the shape, or the vessel God wants us to be.

This is the work of God, and sometimes when we are going through a particularly difficult and painful experience, the Lord will use this experience to refine us, and make us more like Himself.

In the first book by Peter, he speaks of our faith being tested, so that it becomes imperishable, undefiled, and unfading 'so that the genuineness of your faith, more precious than gold, which though perishable is tested by fire, may redound to praise and glory and honour at the revelation of Jesus Christ.'[16]

It is as we go through difficult times the dross is removed from our nature by the work of God, just as gold when heated by fire in a cauldron, all the dross and impurities will come to the top to be scooped away.

When we have been through an experience with the Lord and He has strengthened our faith, and done a deep work within us we must not boast about these things to others. We may pray that the fruits of the Spirit will be attained by the presence of God working

---

[16] 1 Peter 1 vv 7-8.

within us. If the Lord by His grace and mercy perfects these fruits of the Spirit within us, so we attain a gentle and quiet spirit. He will know that together with Him we are truly available for whatever He has planned for us.

We must remember and take comfort in the words of King David in Psalm 139:

> *Thou knowest me right well;*
> *My frame was not hidden from you when I was being made*
> *in secret*
> *Intricately wrought in the depths of the earth.*
> *Thy eyes beheld my unformed substance;*
> *In Thy book were written every one of them,*
> *the days that were formed for me,*
> *when as yet there was not one of them.*

It is always such a wonder when we realise that God knew us even before we were born, and He knows everything about us, and whatever will befall us.

If the days are difficult, and we are feeling utterly distracted, it is always such a comfort to be able to say: 'The Lord knows what I am going through, and all He wants me to do is to 'Forgive' if that is part of the cause of the problem. There is a very comforting verse in Roman's 8: 'He can turn everything to good for those who love Him.' One of the gifts that we might acquire at these difficult times is the gift of Humility, from which surely the other gifts of love, joy, peace, patience, kindness, goodness, faithfulness, gentleness and self-control will follow.

Love Divine

Paul also tells us that we should pray for these gifts, but love should be our first priority. The Lord will give these gifts as we need them. The gifts and fruits of the Spirit are only manifested in the eyes of others and not in the eyes of the one adorned. The promise of God to us is that He will continue this work within us till we are refined like gold and fashioned like silver.

Many years ago we had a young girl living with us. When she was in her early teens her parents' marriage had broken down. Her young sister went to live with her Granny, her brother was old enough to go into the army, but no one wanted Linda in her teens. Her life went downhill rapidly. Fortunately when she was in London, living on the streets, a Christian befriended her. She took Linda to her church and there this unwanted young woman started a new life with the Lord. She never lost this love and was always drawing pictures of the cross and the empty tomb, but because of lack of ministry and the dreadful rejections she had experienced in her life she fell away again and ended up in a psychiatric hospital. After several attempts at taking her own life she eventually came to live with us. There was no doubt that she knew and loved the Lord. One day she was making herself a new skirt, and when she was having difficulty putting in the zip, she suddenly threw the garment down onto the floor exclaiming, 'I have no patience to do this!' After a moment my son teased her, 'You have, Linda. One of the gifts of the Spirit is patience,' whereupon (not surprisingly) she flounced upstairs to her room. After a little while, proving her love and the grace of the Lord, she came back downstairs, picked up her sewing and the zip went in beautifully. It was a lesson I have always remembered.

God in His graciousness gives us these gifts. We need to call upon them and use them for His glory and Kingdom of God.

How meaningful are these words from a favourite hymn from *The Book of Hours* of 1514.

God be in my head, and in my understanding;
God be in my eyes and in my looking;
God be in my mouth, and in my speaking;
God be in my heart; and in my thinking;
God be at my end, and at my parting.

The maid continues with her searching for her Beloved.

V.12: While the King was on His couch, my nard gave forth its fragrance.

We continue to follow the life of the maid, and see how the Lord is so lovingly encouraging her to walk with Him. She is ready to live her life for her Beloved, and He is beginning to see the grace and beauty and humility upon her. He has upheld her in her eager search, as she hastens forward toward the sound of His voice she eventually finds His tent where He is eating. She steps toward her Beloved and as she moves forward He invites her to sit with Him and eat with Him; an informal yet intimate gesture reminding us of His words in the book of Revelation Chapter 3: 'If you open the door (of your life to me) I will come in and sup with you.'

Love Divine

There is a famous painting by Holman Hunt showing Jesus standing amongst weeds and rough grass outside a closed door. He is holding a lamp filled with light and is knocking on the door. There is no latch on the outside so He cannot open the door Himself. It is a wonderful picture of Jesus as the light of the world, knocking on the door of our life, that we must open up to let Him come inside to our life. He will never make our knees bow; we must always ask Him to come into our lives.

I remember the summer when the whole of our family independently began to walk closely with the Lord, and I remember thinking how wonderful for the children to start this their new lives while their future was opening up before them. I always believed even from a young child, but I did not *know* Him. After 53 years of marriage my husband died. Of course I miss him, but I am also comforted by the thought that he is in heaven with the Lord. He had been ill, and now he is out of pain and discomfort and with all the saints in Eternity. I am very grateful for our family and the good friends and comfort that I have where I live, but I know the best is yet to be.

The lovely Christian mezzo-soprano Katherine Jenkins sings such a simple song with a great depth of meaning:

Do not stand at my grave and weep,
I am not there, I do not sleep
I am a thousand winds that blow,
I am the diamond glint on snow

Do not stand at my grave and cry
I am not there. I did not die.[17]

The Lord does not invite us to prepares a formal, specially cooked meal for him, using the best silver and crystal, but to have a simple meal when we can chat and talk and get to know one another. He has brought the maid up to His table, and He invites her to listen to his voice and follow all that He has to tell her. She finds the peace of continual communion and close fellowship with Him. It is in these times when we meditate and feed upon Him, our souls are nourished by the deep meanings and truths, which He opens up to our hearts.

The maid continues to show her delight in the Lord.

While the King was on His couch,
My nard gave forth its fragrance.

The spikenard or nard, is a precious, fragrant and most costly ointment that is usually kept in an alabaster box, which must be broken before the fragrance is released. One of the most meaningful stories in the Bible is of Mary Magdalene who broke her box of nard to anoint the feet of Jesus and wipe them dry with her hair. It was a most loving, humble act of devotion before our Lord went to the cross, and I like to think too that the scent of that perfume stayed with Him and maybe comforted Him during His trial and eventual death.

---

[17] Do Not Stand at My Grave and Weep (1932) by Mary Elizabeth Frye.

Love Divine

Many years ago I was going to a meeting to speak to a group of ladies. I was using the text and the example of Mary who broke open her precious box – so giving her most precious possession to Him.

When I was shopping before the evening meeting, I went to a perfumery to enquire the price of their most expensive perfume that they sold, and they told me it was called *Joy* by Jean Patou. I was told the price was £70 for a tiny bottle. I asked if I could have a spray to experience the perfume, but instead of spraying my wrist, the perfume was sprayed onto a special card, which afterwards I slipped into my Bible to use as a visual aid during the talk. For several months afterwards when I opened my Bible I always smelt that wonderful fragrance and remembered Mary who loved the Lord so much. She gave her all for Jesus, and I also realised how Jesus must have been comforted by the perfume as He went through the trial and trauma of the cross a few days later. I like to believe that through all the centuries Jesus has been comforted and smiled to Himself as we in turn give our lives to Him.

To continue the theme of perfume which is such a speciality in the Song:

V.13: My beloved is to me a sachet of myrrh,
resting between my breasts.

I read of an elderly translator who quite charmingly used these words to describe this verse: 'A little bundle made of myrrh which doth always abide.' Not only does the maid open her jar of

Spikenard but she speaks of the myrrh between her breasts. In Eastern countries much is made of costly oils and perfumes, which the women conceal in little bags of aromatic herbs or a small cruse of oil between their breasts.

Myrrh is not only fragrant, but it is bitter; the bitterness is an emblem of the suffering that the Lord experienced in His life on earth. Maybe the maid is referring to the all-inspiring bittersweet character of love.

It was also used as a spice, a preservative and an antiseptic. As early as in Exodus 30 vv 23-33 the Old Testament tells us that myrrh was used in the compounding of Israel's anointing oil, as well as prized as a perfume.

The maid is beginning to identify with Her Lord, and to understand why He left His home in glory to pay the price for our sins.

She keeps these thoughts and the revelations that the Lord gives her deep in her heart. As we partake with Him in His death, and yield to the cross and all that Jesus wants to change within our souls, so we are refreshed and begin to attract others to the giver of all life.

V.14: My Beloved is to me as a cluster of henna flowers,
from the vineyards of En Gedi.

The henna flowers are heavy with fragrance and hang in beautiful cream white clusters against their bright green leaves. The flowers and leaves present such a richness of perfume and diversity of colour and beauty, that she sees them as a fitting emblem of Christ, who embraces all the power and wonderful attributes of the Godhead. 'For in Him dwells all the fullness of the Godhead.'

The word 'Henna' in the Hebrew means the 'ransom price', and He is our 'Ransom Price.' Only our Lord God, in all His fullness and perfection, could pay the ransom price to redeem our souls. We must put away the vile weeds, the thistles and nettles of our flesh and put on the aroma of Christ, through His love and grace. Nicodemus, the Jewish priest and member of the Jewish ruling council went to see Jesus in the middle of the night, and asked Jesus about his faith and the things that he had heard. His extreme wealth was known throughout the whole of Jerusalem. He gave his sister a million dinars as a dowry, and his niece received 400 dinars a month to replenish her perfume basket, such was the place of perfume held as a necessity or luxury in the first century.

There is a verse Genesis 5 v 24 says simply 'Enoch walked with God.' What a wonderful epitaph to be written in the Bible, an epitaph we should all like to attain.

The test of our life is not how we behave in the exceptional moments of our life, but how we react in the ordinary times, when there is nothing tremendous or exciting going on. The test is how we behave when we are not in front of the footlights.

It was said of Jesus, and He said Himself 'Everything I do is what the Father tells me.' In other words He is completely at one with His Father. Our life should be completely at one with Him in our natural way of thinking and doing. Not the sort of piety that denies the natural life that is not of God but the life that we know our Father in heaven would delight in.

Becoming a monk, nun or hermit will not make us holy unless God has specifically touched our heart to live and worship Him in that way. Raising a family if you are married, often with a full time job, plus supporting and working in your local church, puts much pressure on our lives, and is often where God polishes the pearl within us. I feel too so much for those who are misplaced, and homes and lives destroyed through tragedy, or the greed of man, surely God must have a special place in His heart for them. It must be so difficult to trust God in such situations and not become bitter and discontented. One can't help being touched, and to admire folk from the many places in the world where people have been destroyed and rejected and yet have such peace and radiate Christ in their demeanour. So often they have nothing, lacking even the basic necessities such as clean water or a bowl of rice, and still never deny the Lord. The Negro Spiritual songs sing so simply of the faith of those who were forced onto slavery.

A prayer: 'Lord Jesus, please give me the grace and love to do that, to be myself without any sham or flamboyant religiosity as I walk with you. Please give me the love and compassion of yourself to uplift and pray for those who are in the devastation, and destruction, living through a disaster, and for those who work to bring comfort out of the chaos. Give all the strength and compassion, as they work amongst the great disasters that strike against us in this world.' Amen.

Love Divine

When we hear or read about the suffering of others, to pray, perhaps give financially, and then to offer up the situation to God, seems so often to be the only answer for many of us.

The Beloved again speaks words of comfort to the maid, which anyone of us who is endeavouring to walk closely with the Lord, and is desirous of becoming more like Jesus Christ, should remember and be obedient to all that He ask of us. We must remember Christ's words to us are not dependent on how we feel, but what is going on deep in our hearts.

Vv.15-17: Behold you are beautiful, my love,
Behold you are beautiful
Your eyes are doves.'

These are the words of the Lord as He speaks to the maid. This is not the beauty that the world would see. It is the inward beauty of one who has begun to know Jesus as the Son of God, and whose wish and desire is to follow Him. The maid is beginning to understand something of the work of the cross and the price that Jesus paid as told to us in Philippians 2 v 5:

Have this mind among yourselves, which is yours in Christ
Jesus, who, though He was in the form of God,
Did not count equality with God a thing to be grasped,
But emptied Himself, taking the form of a servant,
Being born in the likeness of men.

These words also speak of the desires of His heart written in His saintly prayer to God His Father in John's Gospel Ch.17:

As Thou didst send me into the world, so I have sent them.
And for their sake I consecrate myself that they also may be
consecrated in truth. I do not pray for these only, but also
for those who believe in me through the word, that they
may all be one, even as thou, Father art in me and I in thee,
that they also may be in us, so that the world may believe
that thou has sent me.

As we read these words we can only but humbly re-consecrate our lives to the Lord. God has provided that as we behold the glory of the Lord, and endeavour to follow Him we shall be changed into His likeness, and become a fellow heir with Jesus Christ. This was the supreme purpose of God creating us, so that we could live our life with Him, and know Him personally in our hearts.

God has provided that, as we behold the glory of the Lord, so we shall be changed into His likeness.

O Lord, you have searched me and you know me.
You know when I sit down and when I rise up;
You perceive my thoughts from afar.
You discern my going out and my lying down,
You are familiar with all my ways,

Love Divine

Before a word is on my tongue
Lo, Lord, you know it completely.[18]

As we grow in our relationship with Jesus, we so often do find that before we have spoken a prayer, He will give us the answer. Jesus sees the secrets of our heart and knows all our especial longings. We must hold His words deep within us, and echo David's prayer at the end of this Psalm.

Search me, O God, and know my heart
Test and know my anxious thoughts,
See if there is any offensive way in me
And lead me in the way everlasting.

Her Beloved continues to encourage her, and to tell her how He sees her.

He speaks to the maid of her beauty. The inner beauty of one who has begun to know the Lord, and whose wish and desire is to follow Him.

V.15: Behold you are beautiful,
Your eyes are doves.

The bride of the Lamb does not walk with outstretched neck and wanton eyes as is spoken of the daughters of Zion. Her eyes are not wandering to and fro in infidelity to her Beloved, but they are chaste, and constant. They are not only like the eyes of the

---

[18] Psalm 139 vv 1-6

dove, but are as doves. Of all the descriptions used to describe the character of the maid, this is one of the most expressive. The dove is always constant to one mate, and there is such a love and devotion between them that is not found in any other bird. I am told that if they quarrel, they make up with a love and intelligence that is not found in any other creature except man. We are not told that her eyes are not like a hawk, or hooded like a bird of prey but she looks to her Lord with wide-open eyes, untouched by slumber or heaviness. The Holy Spirit is often pictured as a white dove and He always points us to Jesus.

She is not looking behind her as Lot's wife did, she is not casting one glance over her shoulder at the world and regretting things and relationships that she has given up. If our hearts are satisfied to be fair in the eyes of our Beloved, though we ourselves feel black and unlovely in the eyes of all others, we shall become much fairer to Him; and His words of approval will warm our hearts.

Matthew 6 v 22 tells us that

The eye is the lamp of the body
So if your eye is sound, your whole body will be full of
light.

The maid remembers how the sun has scorched her when she was tending the vineyards of the world, and she knows that without Him there is no beauty upon her. She desires the Lord's beauty to be of the nature of Jesus upon herself. She understands more about why He came to the earth, and the price He paid for all our sins.

Love Divine

She realises that she might eventually wear the white robes of His righteousness that He bestows upon her.

The Beloved, perhaps recognising her doubts, speaks again to her:

V.17: Behold, you are beautiful my Beloved, Truly beautiful,
Our couch is green, the beams of our house are cedar, our rafters are pine.

At one time the only colour used in a hospital theatre other than white was green. It was believed that as green is a relaxing colour; it could be used to help surgeons relax and concentrate during long hours of surgery. Green is also often used for furnishing homes.

I am sure because of the vision of the beautiful refreshing countryside, is maybe one of the reasons that the 23rd psalm is so well known and liked,

The Lord is my shepherd, I shall not want; he makes me to lie down in green pastures- he restores my soul.

The beams of cedar and the rafters of pine speak of the humanity and death of Jesus. The cedar is an emblem of the pure spotless manhood of Christ, it is the hardest most durable wood, too hard for any worm to burrow into or rot or destroy, this also is true of the fragrant red fir. These two kinds of wood are here used to symbolise Jesus Christ and His redemptive work.

Therefore, He had to be made in every way like his brethren, so that he might become a merciful and faithful high priest in the service of God, to make expiation for the sins of the people.[19]

This house of cedar and fir is not only His house but also our house, for we are no longer strangers and sojourners, but we are fellow citizens with the saints. Fellow heirs of the household of God being built upon the foundation of the apostles and prophets, with Jesus Christ himself being the chief cornerstone.

---

[19] Hebrews 2 v 17.

Love Divine

CHAPTER TWO

In this chapter of the Song, the maid answers her Lord, after all the love, and wonderful words that He has spoken to her. She still feels like a tiny lily-of-the-valley, compared to a tall beautiful white perfumed Madonna lily, as she pictures her Lord.

V.1: I am a rose of Sharon, A lily of the valleys.

'Sharon' and the 'valley' were the most fertile districts of the land of Israel, and these words are the response of the maid to the description of her Lord, to herself. He describes her as being beautiful and fair. She recognises that anything that her Beloved does in her life will be the very best and perfect but she sees herself as a tiny lily-of-the-valley. This lily has tiny white bells, with a beautiful and wonderful scent, but the flower is almost completely hidden by the broad fleshy leaves that curl around the blossom. The flowers are almost hidden, but you know they are there by the wonderful scent of the tiny bells. I was reminded of this verse recently when I was weeding and tidying up the rockery in the garden. Some lily-of-the-valley that I had planted amongst other small plants had crept everywhere, appearing amongst the aubrietia, gentians and other tiny creeping plants.

Compared to other lilies she sees herself as a humble lily full of perfume but hidden away.

She pictures her Beloved as a tall upright beautiful white perfumed lily among the brambles and weeds; the perfect One. I have read recently 'that the world shivered when Jesus came upon the earth, because this new baby was the only one who could redeem the earth and everything in it. When Jesus was crucified the world turned black and rocks and mountains split open.'

The maid compares Him to an apple tree among the trees of the wood. Or correctly the translation refers to a citron tree that is evergreen and bears a fruit like a large lemon in the midst of a wood of deciduous trees that are bare and looking dead in the winter. The evergreen citrus tree would be tall and stately in comparison. She is willing and delighted to sit in His shadow and reflect on all His words and receive His gifts that He bestows upon her. She must be tender, worthy in His worthiness, humble before God and the world and then she will grow more beautiful as a child of God. It is in the valleys of humility, of gentleness and self control that she can become more like her Beloved. He emptied Himself of His glory so we must be emptied of all that will hinder us carrying out the will of God.

V.4: He brought me into His banqueting house, and His banner over me was love.

Many people refer to every blessing experience, to every anointing and joy as being in the Banqueting House, but that is like comparing a small pond to the Atlantic Ocean. In the whole of the Song of Solomon, this is the only time the Banqueting House of the Lord is mentioned. The words refer to a special experience that the Lord promises us in heaven. It is a foretaste of the revelation of Himself and His everlasting love that only Eternity can fully reveal. Sometimes a new Christian may sense this overwhelming experience of love, or the Lord might want to especially anoint His child to confirm the special pathway that he is taking them.

St. Paul speaks of the time when he was lifted up 'to even to the third Heaven into Paradise, and heard unspeakable words that it is not lawful for man to utter.' We are told by reason of the exceeding greatness of the revelations he received from God, he also acquired a 'thorn in the flesh' that he might not be exalted too much. Paul must have had an extraordinary love and relationship with Jesus to endure all the terrible shipwrecks, beating and imprisonments, often lying in chains with guards standing over him, and nowhere in his writings are any signs of complaint or the word 'Why?'.

The maid sees the banner floating over her, the banner of love, with such words as 'We love because He first loved us,' 'While we were yet weak, Christ died for the ungodly' or 'I have loved you with an everlasting love'. These are all the words of Jesus, and sometimes we need to read them and meditate upon them, applying them specifically to ourselves. Not only does the banner of Christ flow over us to show that we have become His through His great love and the work that He continues to do within us.

Many times when the authorities would have taken Jesus, He slipped out of their hands, maybe because of the fear amongst those who would harm Him. It was God, and His unseen banner over Jesus that brought fear to His enemies. When it was God's time that His son should die, it appeared to some that God was not with Him, so the fear that restrained those who wanted to kill Him left the authorities and attackers, and they took Him to the cross.

Love Divine

Even on the cross when the face of the Father turned away from Him, because His Son became not only as sin, but He became sin, as He took on His shoulders the price of every sin that has been committed, the sin of you and me which a Holy God could not look upon. The Roman soldiers shouted and derided him, 'He trusted in God, let Him deliver Him now.'

If we are walking in humility and obedience in the night and in the day; in the dark places; in the light places in our life, the banner of the love of the Lord is always over us, and we need to cling to it and always keep it in sight.

The maid is still yearning for her Beloved, she wants to understand more:

V.5: Strengthen me with raisins, refresh me with apples;
for I am faint with love.

She desires that her relationship will go ever deeper with her Lord. There is a quality about love that we feel that we can never truly express.

As the deer pants for streams of water, so my soul pants for
you O God,
My soul thirsts for God, the living God. When can I go and
meet with God?
My tears have been my food day and night,
While men say to me all day long, where is your God?[20]

---

[20] Psalm 42 vv 1-3.

'For I am faint with love,' sighs the maiden, which is like saying 'I want all or nothing.' Is it better for lovers if they cannot be united, not to love at all? It is a special quality of love not to be stationary, to always be ready to serve that love, so that there is no fear of Love diminishing. For it is the unrest, the sickening pain of separation away from the beloved that we then begin to fear that the love will not be returned and consummated.

V.6: His left arm is under my head, and His right arm embraces me.

This support and embracing of the Lord's arms is often the only thing that keeps us from falling away. It may be through bad news or sudden illness, or a situation that you might find yourself in, or it may be through criticism or jealousy. Yet you know that God is still on the throne. Sometimes, a difficult situation makes us want 'to jump off a bridge' and yet all the time we are aware that He does know what is happening. We are held firm in His embrace while His right arm leads us and guides us and gives us the strength to see through the difficulty. So often after such times we can say 'I know more of Him through these circumstances, and no-one can destroy that and take His love away'.

Let us always take our strength and peace from the warm embrace of His left arm, let us yield to His right hand even though the way forward may not be easy. Let Him hold us fast to pour into us the oil to soothe us, and then when the purifying and moulding furnace through which we have come we will we will find that we have been cleansed from dross in our life and we can thank God

Love Divine

for what He has done in us. We also then find that through the experience we are closer to Him, and really begin to understand the verse in John 12 v 24:

'He who loses his life for my sake will gain it. I tell you the truth, unless a grain of wheat falls into the ground and dies, it remains a single seed, but if it dies it produces many seeds'

This verse causes us to pray:

'Dear Lord, I pray that I will know more of your life and love, I recommit my life to you, knowing that whatever the future holds for me, you will always strengthen and uphold me with the warmth and guiding of your embrace.'

The maid speaks to those around her,

V.7: Daughters of Jerusalem, I charge you by the gazelles and the does of the field: Do not arouse or waken love until it so desires.

Although we may experience 'mountain peaks' of revelation, which God gives us when we are brought into a deeper and closer relationship with Him. He does not intend that the experience should be temporary, but to be permanent and increasing within us. How vivid is the warning the maid gives to others, using the gazelles in the heights and the quiet silent does in the field to express the care we must take not to grieve the Holy Spirit. Nothing must cause a barrier between the Lord, and ourselves and thus hinder the Lord working within us. Whatever changes the Lord may make in our nature and attitude, it is for the whole of our life, and will be as the character of Jesus.

74

As careful as the hunter follows the doe so we must live and work. No animal is as difficult to hunt as the doe or hind. Only the trained hunter knows how carefully he must take every step if he wishes to capture one of these animals. It is with great care we must walk not to disturb the Lord with a careless moment or heedless action, or even because we are taken up with something even though it might be some necessary duty. Many times we seek for a deeper walk with the Lord and when it is granted us in good measure, we immediately begin to rejoice over it with such self-elation, that, when we look, He appears to have left us, not because He has moved away, but because through the delight we have uplifted ourselves, not God.

We know how careful we are not to grieve or upset someone whom we truly love, and with whom we want to remain in a close loving relationship.

One of the most precious lessons and most solemn warnings to be found in the Song of Solomon is drawn from the Lord's sudden disappearance from the vision and presence of the maid. He may be with her in such intimacy and presence, and almost immediately He seems to have gone. So it is with our Lord in His teaching with us. Maybe we have not valued the dealings of God, and the indwelling of Jesus Christ and the Holy Spirit as we should. We may have taken His gifts just as something we are to enjoy, and we have let them become commonplace, instead of always holding them in awe, worship, and thankfulness.

God does not cleanse us more and more from sin, when we are in the light and walking in the light, we are cleansed from all sin. It

Love Divine

is always a question of obedience and repentance, and then instantly our relationship with the Lord is restored. So it is with the revelations and gifts from God, they are all sealed until they are opened to be used in obedience to Him. We will never acquire them by philosophy or thinking. Immediately we obey, a flash of light seems to come and we begin to understand and are aware that God has given us something special to use with Him. We must let the truths of God work in us, by soaking ourselves in Him, and not by worrying ourselves into it. When we obey God in the thing that He shows us, we then so quickly realise that another truth has opened up to us.

We may read books and books on the work of the Holy Spirit, yet five minutes being obedient to what He says, suddenly we find everything becomes as clear as a sunbeam. Just as a cobweb can shelter the grass from the dew, so our obedience and turning towards Him can bring us closer into His presence.

V.9: The voice of my beloved,
look, here He comes,
Leaping across the mountains
Bounding over the hills.
My beloved is like a gazelle or a stag,
Look there He stands behind our wall
Peering through the lattice.

The maid recognises the soft gentle voice of her Beloved in the stillness, as He comes before her.

David's Psalm 22 refers to Jesus as 'The Hind of the Dawn,' it is one of the most prophetic and agonising of the psalms, which tells of the cost of the One who came from Heaven to earth to pay the price and to conquer the sins of us all. In the Hebrew the word for 'hind' and 'hart' are the same. Our Lord was the 'Hind of the Morning,' the One who came as the Light if the world.

He leapt over all the mountains of sin and condemnation, of God's wrath and displeasure, and He came to bring peace and reconciliation, to bring redemption to a lost and sin-cursed world.

The maid knows He is not far away, but she is standing back, waiting for Him to come to her.

V.9: Look, there he stands
Behind our wall, gazing in at the windows,
Peering through the lattice.

It was the Lord who took away the wall that stood between fallen humanity and God. It was He who took away the wall that shuts out the people from God and His promises; and in Himself he made one new man of both Jew and Greeks through peace and reconciliation on the cross. He also broke down the wall between God and each individual. In His love He comes to each individual, to our own wall and lattice which separated each one of us personally with the barrier of sin, from a Holy God. It is always our wall and not His wall because it is built from our sin and unbelief, and we need to continually watch and see that we do not build it up again.

Love Divine

There is also the wall of captivity and refusal that we can build around ourselves when we imprison ourselves against further rejection or fear of abuse. It is a wall that we build around us so that we feel secure and hidden from the world. The hurt and pain is still there deep down inside us, which we continually push down and hide away from our thoughts. We can even try to 'forget' the hurts and pain and what caused them, but unfortunately when we are in certain innocent situations we react badly because the pain and hurt are still there, registered in the brain. These unfortunate reactions come back into our life just as a beach ball that is pushed down into the water will always bounce back up again. I heard a psychiatrist say that our mind is like an iceberg, one-tenth above the surface of the water, but nine tenths buried in the deep waters hidden away. It is only the Lord who knows these deep hurts and rejected pain, and He can gently through the work of the Holy Spirit bring them back to the surface so that through prayer and trust in Him we can be healed and restored.

I always find the loving touching way that the Lord speaks to Peter in John 16, so very special.

John tells us in Chapter 21 of his gospel, that after the Resurrection, Jesus went to the beach where He knew the disciples would be fishing, knowing that they would most probably be feeling very despondent. He made a fire on the beach and called to the disciples to bring some fish for breakfast. They had not caught any all night, but the voice calling to them from the beach suggested that they should throw the nets in on the right hand side of their boats. Immediately the nets were full to overflowing, without being torn, and the disciples realised that it was Jesus on the beach.

When the disciples realised the 'Voice' was their Master, they all rushed to get to Him quickly, particularly Peter who always wanted to be the first everywhere. Except this time the passage tells us that for a moment, he paused to cover himself up, and then ran onto the beach. This covering was like a tiny wall that Peter was erecting around himself, because he instantly remembered the three times that he had denied that he knew Jesus, and he felt there might be a shadow in their relationship. The time was early morning, it was not yet fully light, Jesus had lit a fire, and the half-light was similar to the time when standing round a fire Peter had denied Jesus. After breakfast Jesus called Peter aside, and three times He asked Peter if he loved Him, and three times Peter affirmed his love for the Lord, and three times he knew he was forgiven, and Jesus reminded Peter again of his calling to follow Him, and bring others into the Kingdom.

Jesus knew that unless Peter experienced grace, and knew he was forgiven for the three times he had denied the Lord, he would carry the hurt and pain of that memory in his heart, and so would never be the open fearless upright man of God, Jesus knew him to be. In the book of Acts Chapter 2, Peter, with this peace within himself that there was now no barrier between himself and the Lord, spoke loudly and clearly to the assembly of people. Addressing the Jews and all those in Jerusalem he explained again who Jesus was, and told the crowds that they all had received the Holy Spirit that Jesus had promised. He then finished this

Love Divine

wonderful open-air sermon in the crowded streets of Jerusalem with the words 'Let all the house of Israel know assuredly that God has made Him both Lord and Christ, this Jesus whom you crucified.'

Hardly the words of a broken disheartened man.

Verse 9 also tells us that the Lord stands, and waits outside the wall of the maid's life. He is waiting to lead the maid further into her new life with Him.

V.10: Arise my beautiful one, and come with me,
 See, the winter is past; the rains are over and gone.
 Flowers appear on the earth,
 The season of singing has come.
 The cooing of doves is heard in our land.
 The fig tree forms its early fruit
 The blossoming vines spread their fragrance.
 Arise my love, my beautiful love,
 Come with me.

We may experience a time when the Lord offers us something and instead of rising up and going with Him, we are not prepared to leave everything that we know, and to posses that which He wants to shows us. Maybe we have been seeking a new direction in our lives, and when our thoughts turn in a way that we were not expecting, we are not prepared to leave our ease and comfort and our own wills in place of His wish for us. It is when we first hear His voice, maybe to suggest a new, or He may want us to ask someone if they will forgive us for a misdeed and we need to say that we are sorry. If the Lord asks us to react to a circumstance in a way that we find difficult, we can always ask for His grace and help in the situation, or we may ask Him to confirm this new way, but we do need to be prepared to rise up and obey Him. He may call us and speak to us many times, all the time waiting for us to acknowledge Him, till eventually His voice will grow fainter and fainter, so that when we do respond we may not find Him so quickly. If we still find the situation difficult because we feel that the situation was so extreme to even consider, we can ask the Lord to give us the grace to begin to obey.

I remember at a conference an attractive young woman asking me to pray for her. Her face was so withdrawn and strained that I guessed it had been a feeling of desperation that she had even come to me. She couldn't even talk about what had happened to her, but she did say that she was experiencing a strain in her marriage through this problem. I felt the only answer to whatever had happened, was to ask God for His help for her to forgive the perpetrators, and we prayed together for her to want to open her pain to Jesus Christ. He knows her, loves her and wants her to be healed from the pain. The next morning after the Holy Communion service the last place at the table for lunch was opposite to where she was sitting, I hardly recognised this beautiful young women, her eyes were sparkling, she was smiling and relaxed, and as I silently thanked the Lord for His healing in her life.

He does know the deep desires of our heart and will gently lead us towards Him.

Love Divine

The Lord continues to speak with love and comfort to the maid-

V.1: .See, the winter is past, the rain is over and gone
The flowers appear on the earth, the season of singing has
come,
The cooing of doves is heard in our land,
The fig tree forms its early fruit
The blossoming vines spread their fragrance.
Arise, come my love, my beautiful, come with me.

Winter in this verse is referring to the old dispensation and the law of the covenant, which is written in the Old Testament. These were laws that had no power to bring to life dead souls who ignored the word of God. The great patriarchs believed and obeyed. Sometimes we read that the Spirit of God fell upon the people, but the ushering in of the new dispensation of grace, which in these verses are symbolised by the spring, is the birth of Jesus and the new personal life that the Lord Jesus offers us, if we follow Him. The law of God has never been fulfilled except by Jesus Christ. That which man could not do by himself, Jesus Christ a perfect man but also the Son of God, came and paid the price of our sin when He went to Calvary. All the darkness and winter of the wrath of a Holy God that we read in the Old Testament and the condemnation, which rested upon man was paid for, and the barrier lifted between a Holy God and us by the one perfect sufficient sacrifice of Jesus Christ.

These verses in the this canticle of the Song are so beautifully descriptive with so much meaning that one feels they are worthy of days of meditation.

The poetry and wonderful descriptions of nature and the earth in the whole of the Bible, the deep truths and learning makes it seem impossible to pick out special verses, but it also makes it such a personal precious book for everyone of us, whether a scholar or a simple child. I started to look through the book of Job, that wonderful old man of God. Then I felt I must turn to Ecclesiastes, or Genesis, the psalms and proverbs, which are so relevant for today. Both the Old and New Testaments point to the wonders of poetry and language and these verses are a picture of the soul who has been dead in unbelief, full of darkness and fruitlessness. When life seems bleak and all is darkness and cold in the midwinter, it is difficult to see the beauty and sparkle even in the darkest of days. Then when the rays of sun begin to warm the earth, and the rain begins to break up the soil, the feelings of death and decay begin to roll away. We feel the nearness of Spring as small shoots begin to show in the gardens, and the warmth of the sun quickens the seemingly dead trees. The whole earth comes alive and our souls respond with joy and laughter.

I always find it such a joy every sunny morning, when after the birds have raided the bird table they sit in twos and threes on top of a tall hedge with their breast feathers all puffed up facing the warm sun. They are making the most of the warm Scottish sun.

Spring always seems to be such a wonderful time of the year, heralding all the glory and promises of Summer. Even the smallest trees are full of pink and white blossom, and in the U.K. the landscape is dotted with Van Gogh yellow rape, interspersed with the blue green wheat and early crops. The air seems to be full of diving swallows, and busy house martins almost flying right into the windows as they build their nest of mud in the eaves. The hedgerows are full of psychedelic bluebells and brilliant pink campions, flowering in the lively warmth of the air that is so unlike the heat of a hot August, but now gently caresses us as we go about our daily business.

The picture of seeds falling into the ground by the farmers sowing, and the trees putting out buds and shoots which will eventually produce fruit reminds us of our new life that we can have with the Lord. The Beloved uses them to encourage the maid in a gentle, beautiful way to realise the new life that He wants her to experience.

This new life in us that we know now, and which Jesus gave up His life, so that we can now receive it, will also cost us our life. If we give ourselves to Him and His sovereign way of life, we will receive the peace that passes all understanding that will never leave us.

The seed dying when it falls into the soil is a metaphor for the new life which the maid will have with her betrothed, and the secret of that life is dying to self and living for her Beloved, putting Him first, and being available to serve and help other people.

It is interesting too that the phrase 'The rain is over and gone' referring to the Old Covenant, does not mean that we should ignore the Old Testament. It is still very relevant to our lives. Indeed we cannot but be inspired by the lives of those who believed and followed their God, without the truth of the New Testament. Moses was just an ordinary guy who stuttered, but who believed in God, and was obedient to Him. Moses escaped the slaughter of all new babies, by Herod, and ended up in the palace of the Pharaoh to eventually become the ruler who led his people the Israelites out of Egypt and into the Promised Land. They spent 40 years wandering in the deserts, the people complaining bitterly all the time against God. As we continue to read the lives of all the Patriarchs and men and women, who believed and trusted in their God we can always be inspired. They didn't have the assurance and know the forgiveness that we can experience in our lives, or have the encouragement and inspiration from the lives of the Saints, throughout all the centuries. They were just ordinary men and women who believed and trusted in their God.

These verses in the Song are a picture of the soul who has been dead in unbelief, full of darkness. When life seems bleak and cold like the midwinter, it is difficult to see the beauty and sparkle even in the darkest of days. Then when the rays of the sun begin to warm the earth and the rain begins to break up the soil, so will feelings of death and decay begin to roll away with hope and joy. We become aware of small shoots that begin to appear in the earth, and the warmth of the sun quickens the seemingly dead trees, as the tiny leaves begin to appear. The whole earth seems to gradually come alive and our own souls respond with joy.

Love Divine

Recently I was driving home just when the sun was setting and was very low in the sky. I had to stop the car and just look at the spectacular sky, and the tremendous light of the setting sun with the iridescent vibrant colours affecting the countryside for miles. The bright glow of the mixture of fluorescent orange touched with the blood red of crimson of the setting sun silently lighting up the dim but soft blue in the sky. The tall dark trees that had begun to melt into the soft dusky land, dimming the blues and greens in the hills were suddenly lit with an incredible brilliant gold glazing everything in its path. The ancient wall on one side of the road and all the nearby trees and fields recently ploughed with deep furrows on the other side, were all bathed in brilliant gold. I thought I must remember this and try to paint this magical light, but no paints in the hands of even the greatest artist of all time could capture such wonder and brilliance. Feeling tired at the end of a busy day I continued on my way home, again wondering afresh at our creator God, who gives us such a brilliant created world to remind us again of His grace and power that He alone can paint.

As spring comes the first tiny bulbs begin to appear and early buds begin to show upon the bushes and trees. Even though they may as yet be very tiny they are a sign of the promises of God and the flowers and fruit that is yet to come.

The picture of the seeds falling into the prepared ground in the Spring and eventually growing into plants that produce fruit is a picture of the life of the maid as she turns towards her Beloved. John 12 v 24 says:

86

Truly, truly, I say unto you, unless a grain of wheat falls into the earth and dies, it remains alone; but if it dies, it bears much fruit.

He who loves his life will lose it, and he who hates his life in this world will keep it for eternal life.

This seems a harsh verse for those who do not know the Lord, but if you do know and love Him, it is difficult to imagine life without Him. We can always take comfort from His promises and all that He reveals to us. It was a truly blessed time when my husband died, but even though I am lonely without him, it is such a comfort to know for certain where he is, and that one day I shall be with him again.

The Beloved wants the maid to arise from her bed so that she may enter more fully into the life that he wants her to experience with Him. He can already see the beginning of fruit in her life, and changes within her, as he speaks of the fig trees beginning to bear fruit and the blossom on the vines already giving out their fragrance with the promise of the fruit which is to come. He knows that she is encouraging new Christians in their faith, and is also growing in her understanding of her own faith. But He knows that she needs to learn more fully to grow and trust Him.

The Lord beseeches the maid again, demonstrating to us the love that we can experience from the Lord, and how encouraging He is when the world might ridicule and deride us when we seek Him.

Love Divine
V.14: My dove in the cleft of the rock,
In the hiding-places on the mountain side,
Show me your face
Let me hear your voice;
For your voice is sweet and your face is lovely.

Mathew tells us in his Gospel that the moment Jesus died on the cross the earth shook, and the sky was covered in darkness, as the rocks were split open and the tombs were opened up, and many bodies of the saints who had fallen asleep were raised. Such was the tremendous power and strength that was released on the earth.

Though the wind blows and the hurricane sweeps down upon her in her hiding place and the enemy sends out all his power upon her and against her, nothing of the power of evil can overcome the maid because she is hidden away in the Rock. Her life is safe within His life. As she seeks her refuge in Him, in His safe hands, nothing can happen to her that He won't allow, whatever may assail her, He will always give her the grace to withstand all difficulties and problems. She need not fear even though the mountains shake and the seas roar, she knows He is at her right hand and nothing can take Him away from her. It is here in the Rock of the Lord we know that He is always with us. He knows every difficulty that might beset us but He will never ever leave us to go through it alone. We need to ask, confess if that is part of the problem and stay close to Him. All the hardness and suffering are forgotten if we retreat deeper into Him where no one but God is with us. It is not an easy path, but it is wonderful and it becomes more blessed as we begin to fully understand that this pathway on

88

earth is our stairway to Heaven. From weakness and humiliation, to strength and through strength to one day experience glory.

There is a story that some artists were asked to paint a picture of peace. One painted a beautiful yacht sailing in peaceful waters during a most beautiful sunset.

The second artist painted a picture of a beautiful flower showing all the beauty and delicacy and colour of the petals. The third artist painted a picture of a horrendous electric thunderstorm with the sea and rain raging on a tall rock, but in the rock was a deep cleft in which a white dove was peacefully sheltering.

I have always been so impressed when I have read about Christians who have been tortured and beaten and then imprisoned in solitary confinement because they would not deny their faith. Many have testified that at such times they have been able to sing and worship God, and have experienced the most wonderful presence of the Lord with them. Some have even testified that as their conditions worsened and life was more difficult His presence was with them even more powerfully, and with Him survived the most difficult tortuous situations.

I remember hearing Richard Wurmbrand, a playboy turned preacher speak about his imprisonment in Rumania when the country was under Communist rule. He was in prison for 14 years while his jailers tried to force him to confess that he was part of an imperialistic network. In spite of beatings, torture and drugging, his spirit did not break. For two years he was a prisoner in the 'death room'-so called because no other man had left it alive. Also here, too, as a pastor, he found his parish, an unforgettable gallery

Love Divine

of thieves, murderers, saints and sinners who also shared his cell 'until each in turn passed through the gap of death.'[21]

He told of his sadness when he came to the U.K. and America after his release during the 1970s, to find the West so apathetic and indifferent concerning their faith. During the sixties and seventies many laws were passed that seemed not to ignore the Christian faith. However it does seem that since the turn of the Century we are experiencing a movement of the Spirit God over the whole world.

This is the song that David sang when the Lord saved him from his enemies, and the hand of Saul.

The Lord is my rock, my fortress and my deliverer;
My God is my rock, in who I take refuge,
He is my shield, and the horn of my salvation,
And my stronghold.
I call to the Lord who is worthy of my praise
And I am saved from my enemies.[22]

It is in the cleft of the Rock that was opened up at Calvary that we can hide from the plotting of man and the reproach of cruel tongues. If we are misunderstood and unjustly accused or maligned we can hide in the cleft of the rock, we can be hidden with Christ in God.

---

[21] *In God's Underground,* Hodder and Stoughton 1968.
[22] Psalm 18 vv 1-3.

The Beloved is still encouraging the maid to turn more fully to Him.

V.14: Let me see your face. Let me hear your voice, for your voice is sweet, and your face is comely.

It always seems so amazing that Jesus who has done so much for each one of us, even if we are in ignorance of Him, He is always willing to go the extra mile to encourage us if He sees that we are beginning to turn to Him. In His love for us, He always wants our face turned towards Him. He entreats the maid to turn so that He may see her countenance, for it is only when the face of the maid is turned towards Him that He sees her eyes and smile. It is when we are in the steepest, hardest places, when it seems that our very life will go out, and we are tempted to sit down and feel sorry for ourselves, that God draws us closer to Himself. When we are turned Heavenward even in the times of great difficulties that confront us, and we refuse to not just look at the difficulties and trials but look to our Lord, then He begins to transfigure us into His own image. He knows the work that must be done before we are like Him, and are ready to go into the marriage supper of the Lamb. He calls the maid to set her face steadfastly toward Him, to run with patience the race set before her, looking to Himself, the Author and Finisher of our faith. And as we steadfastly obey we will hear His voice say 'Your countenance is beautiful, you are all fair, and there is no spot in you.'

Not only does He want to see her face always turned towards Him, but He wants to see her and hear her always in communion

Love Divine

with Him in prayer, in worship and in praise. He is grieved when she speaks unkind, untrue, gossiping words, words tainted with insincerity and guile, bitterness, envy and jealousy. Even if we can hardly understand that our voice is sweet to the Lord, even when we know His voice is sweet to us, He tells us that a thousand times more is our voice sweeter to Him. And we hear His voice say to us:

'O my dove, you are hiding in the clefts of the rock, come let me see your face, and hear your voice as we travel the pathway together.'

Then we are overcome with joy.

I think that we need to come to a state when we are always aware that He is with us. We can speak to Him in our mind or even chatter to Him during the day.

A few years ago, I was driving my husband and a family friend to see a particular castle. We were in an unfamiliar car, and soon after we had begun the journey I just thought to myself 'Please help me Lord and keep us safe.' After a few miles we were in a most horrific accident, we were hit by a Transit van, which sent us over the central reservation, turned us completely round and upside down, so that our wheels were spinning in the air. The most amazing thing was that none of us were hurt, except our passenger in the back, who had been reading the paper and ended up strapped in but upside down. After an X Ray, he was found to have a crack in his sternum, a small bone in the top of his chest, and when we arrived in hospital he was sitting up in bed eating turkey sandwiches. What amazed me afterwards were all the incredible miracles that happened. A witness saw the crash and took notes, he was the driver of a van I was overtaking, and happened to be a chauffeur for a neighbour of ours who now lived in London. As a chauffeur he had been taught to write everything down in a statement after an accident. A car travelling with Marines stopped to minister first aid to us after we landed on the opposite side of the road, and a police car which had been travelling behind us extricated our upside down guest, who was over 80, through a window. My husband who was in the front passenger seat, which was where the large vehicle hit us was unhurt, and we crawled out of the squashed flattened vehicle together. I had just chatted to the Lord, and He had prepared everything, far more abundantly than we could ever have dreamed. God did not stop the accident; we went through it with His help.

V.15: Catch us the foxes,
the little foxes that spoil the vineyards,
for our vineyards are in blossom.

This is a puzzling verse at this point in the Song. Perhaps it is one more example of the poignancy of love. Just when love seems on the point of fulfilment, casting a romantic spell on nature itself, the maid and her Beloved sense the ominous possibility that subversive forces may threaten their love.

The 'foxes' are 'little,' but they can burrow and gnaw at the roots of the vines, so killing them. They usually are interpreted as the small sins that we commit often unaware that we are, or thinking that they do not count as sins; or example an unhelpful

Love Divine

attitude, an unasked for criticism, a judgmental attitude to another or even a half-truth. But they can cause a barrier as any other sin, especially if we know they are wrong. I once heard a friend say 'I like to keep a short account with the Lord, and my ironing board!'

Her Beloved warns the maid that it is not enough to sit in the garden enjoying the flowers and their fragrance,. It is not enough to know that you have become part of the inheritance of the Saints and have become part of the Kingdom of the Son of God. She must be acting her part in the Kingdom, she must be keeping the vineyard of her own soul,

Her desire must be to be a handmaid for the Lord.

St. Augustine said:

Without God we cannot.
Without us God will not.

The maid is beginning to realise that she must take every fox, or wrong out of her life. The wrong thoughts or attitudes, those small things that we know are wrong but we feel are least important and too insignificant to cause any harm or trouble. It is not the great things in our lives that cause us to fail God the most. When we are challenged with something that is formidable we know that it must be overcome and we draw upon the grace and the power of the Lord to overcome it. These small foxes in our lives may be the habits, words, or our old natural self that have been with us for years; and which are so much part of our lives that we are hardly conscious that they are there at all. We forget that the Lord has given us His Holy Spirit, the Spirit of Truth who will reveal and help us to overcome any wrong so that we may become a true disciple.

I remember a great missionary who worked in Taiwan, coming back to our Church during his furlough. We eagerly looked forward to his message, our congregation was usually 400 plus, with many outreaching activities. Imagine our chagrin as a church when he spoke from the verses in Chapter 2 v 13 in the Song. 'Be aware of the foxes,' he said. 'Even a pencil that you take away that is not yours, will grieve the Spirit within you. Take care with your attitude to others, and how you speak. There must be no pride in anything you do.'

We should aim to attain in our lives the words of Isaiah 61 v 10:

I will greatly rejoice in the Lord,
my soul shall exult in my God;
for he has clothed me with the garments of salvation,
he has covered me with the robe of righteousness,
as a bridegroom decks himself with a garland, and as a
bride adorns herself with her jewels.
For as the earth brings forth its shoots,
And as a garden causes what is sown in it to spring up,
So the Lord God will cause righteousness and praise
To spring forth before all nations.

A prayer: 'O Lord, please keep me close to yourself. I feel that I fall far short of all that you hope from me. I know that I can only be worthy of you by the help and guiding of your Holy Spirit. I

Love Divine

pray for the continual grace of Him that I might be worthy of your love.' Amen.

V.16: My beloved is mine and I am his,
He browses among the lilies.

While the maid was hiding in the clefts of the rock her Beloved has spoken to her in love and assurance, in gentle warning and encouragement. She is assured of her union with Him, which is eternal and indissoluble. Her heart is filled with rest because He is hers; and she is apprehending with Paul in Romans 8 v 38 '…that neither death nor life, nor angels, nor principalities nor things present, nor things to come... will be able to separate us from the love of God in Christ Jesus our Lord.' What a truly wondrous thought, that as far as our relationship is to Him, and His love and care towards us are concerned, our Lord is ours as fully, as preciously, as though He loved and died for each one of us alone.

However, there is still the word 'self' very prevalent in the mind of the maid. In spite of the love and encouragement that the Lord has given her, she still wants his love on her own terms.

'My beloved *is* mine, and *I* am his.'

The words 'My' and 'I' still imply that everything is still on her own terms.

V.16: He pastures His flock amongst the lilies.

The Lord is always amongst His people, and it is the pure in heart that shall see God. He is walking and talking with them. He is in the midst of them as He leads and teaches them, as He pastures His flocks and takes His rest.

V.17: Until the day breaks and the shadows flee, turn my Beloved, be like a gazelle, or a young stag upon rugged mountains.

The maid begins to acknowledge, and to openly realise that 'Until the day breaks and the shadows flee ' – In other words 'forever' the Lord, for all time as we understand it, will always be there, whether it is at first light or the darkest part of the night He will always be there.

The mountains, upon which the Lord passed at his first coming, were the mountains of separation from God, because the divine law of God was continually being broken, and the sentence of death and condemnation was resting upon mankind. These mountains of Bether are divided by deep chasms, symbolic of the gulf of separation, which sin has made between fallen humanity and a Holy God. These mountains of separation are raised many times by indifference or unfaithfulness in us. Why do we not hear His voice more often and more clearly? Is it because we have made mountains of separation by our own thoughts and opinions, and by the wickedness of man?

Love Divine

Why do we not get guidance more easily and perfectly? Maybe it is because we want and really desire to have our own will and go our own way. We may even cause mountains of separation because of our own desire for love of the flesh and the natural, rather than love for Christ and the spiritual world.

CHAPTER THREE

V.1: All night long on my bed I looked for the one my soul loves:
I looked for Him but did not find Him.

This is a repetition of the verse at the end of Chapter Two. She has been waiting through the darkness for the first rays of dawn, which represent the Lords 'presence', but the night of darkness is still around her and her cry at the end of the chapter has not been granted. The love of the bride is burning brightly, she is longing and seeking Him whom her soul loves; she is hungry for Him but she is still in her bed. This may be a sign of her indolence but it does not show indifference because she has been earnestly crying for His presence. It is not however that we find Him when we are indolent and lying in our bed, it is not when we are too unconcerned to get up and seek Him, if we only are prepared to seek Him when we have nothing better to do, when we have a few moments of leisure. It is those who seek with increasing determination that receive the ' exceedingly abundantly far more that they ask or think.' If we want this new relationship we must seek and find him.

V.2: I will get up now and go about the city, through the streets and squares;
I will search for the one my soul loves.
So I looked for Him but did not find Him.

Love Divine

When the maid finds that He does not come to her, she shakes off her indolence and laziness and determines to go out into the streets and broad ways to find Him. She remembers the time when He told her to sit at the feet of the shepherds, and feed her kids by the shepherd's tents. Also that brings back memories to her when through obedience she found Him and was invited to sit at His own table. When we are longing for a greater vision of our Beloved, often a word from a mature Christian will advise us to read a particular book, or to be more committed to attend particular services. He will lead us to those who have gone along the way; those who can guide us into a closer relationship with him and into a clearer revelation of His beauty and grace.

The bride arises to go about the city, to seek Him, in the broad ways, in the streets and the alleys in the city. This literally means the city of Jerusalem, in the city gates where the citizens gathered to transact business, in the assembly or special places of vision and blessing. We must also search for Him in the hidden paths, and undesirable places. He may bring us down step by step until we care for nothing but a deeper revelation of Him. The Lord will not Let us set our minds upon any certain way or place in which He must meet us. He will speak to us at any time no matter what we are doing; sometimes it may be when we are quiet and relaxing in the bath. This for me is often the case.

V.3: The watchman found me as they as they made their rounds in the city.
  'Have you seen the one my heart loves?

The watchman and shepherds found her; it was not the maid who found them. They were the faithful ministers of the Gospel and the ones who look after the sheep; they were looking after the flock and searching for those who were bewildered and in need. Although these faithful shepherds were near enough to direct her it was not until she had passed them that she found her Beloved. We may praise God for all those persons over the years who have pointed us towards our Beloved, those whom we have known and who directed us, who brought us new light, who stirred within us a deeper hunger for God, and who provoked us to holy jealousy and emulation through their godly lives. I remember many faithful souls over the years who led me to a greater hunger for God, and abandonment to do His will and follow Him all the way.

V.4: Scarcely had I passed them when I found the one my heart loves.
I held Him and would not let Him go till I had brought Him to my mother's house.
To the room of the one who conceived me.

How her heart rejoices as she finds Him. She has been searching for Him through the city streets, and now with a burst of sheer joy and worship and love she clings to Him in fear that He will leave her again. There is a slight hint in this verse that perhaps He would go on further after she has found Him, as though He is willing to only be held by that soul who will not take a refusal from Him. How much more would our Beloved abide in us if through diligent search we found Him in greater revelation; and

Love Divine

then through prayer, communion and obedience, we held Him fast and would not let him go. If our hearts were as hungry for Him as pictured here, and we clung to Him so tenaciously would He never vanish from our spiritual vision?

She brings Him into the chambers of her Mother. The bride remembers when she was keeping the vineyards of the world, when the sons of her mother set her to do the work on their lowly tasks, and she consequently neglected her own vineyards. She wants the kinsmen of her own flesh to leave their work in the world, she longs that they too might come to know the vineyards of their own souls. Her heart longs that her Beloved might become their Beloved.

V.5: Daughters of Jerusalem, I charge you by the gazelles
and by the does of the field:
do not arouse or waken love, until it so desires.

This is the same warning that the maid brought to the daughters of Jerusalem in the second chapter and we have considered, but this time there is a change of motive. In Ch. 2 v 7, the bride is concerned that her own joy and rest should not be interrupted; that nothing shall break the fellowship and love that *she* is having with her Beloved. In this chapter she is concerned that nothing shall grieve the Lord or turn Him away before her kinsman receives him, and she is hoping that they too might come to know Him in their lives, and come to know His love and joy. She does not want the daughters of Jerusalem (those who already believe in Him) to disturb Him, or hinder the work of the Holy

Spirit. She is not considering that her own inconsistent living, or her thoughtless insistence that others should always comply with her often selfish desires can disturb and grieve the Holy Spirit.

> *Vv.6-10: Who is this coming up from the desert like a*
> *column of smoke, perfumed with myrrh and incense,*
> *Made from all the spices of the merchant?*
> *Look! It is Solomon's carriage, escorted by sixty warriors,*
> *the noblest of Israel, all of them wearing the sword,*
> *all experienced in battle, each with his sword by his side*
> *prepared for the terrors of the night.*
> *King Solomon made for himself the carriage;*
> *he made it of wood from Lebanon.*
> *Its posts he made of silver, its base of gold.*
> *Its seat was upholstered in purple, its interior lovingly*
> *inlaid by the daughters of Jerusalem.*

We can read these verses as a picture of Jesus coming among the people, putting aside His home in Glory to come and redeem the world. Or we can read them as a description of Christ coming to each one of us, paying the price for all our sins, and drawing us into a personal relationship with Him.

These verses are an exclamation of wonder and joy, told by those who saw the procession coming up through the wilderness. Such glory and magnificence, such a golden glittering chariot, perfumed with incense, myrrh and wonderful spices, with a column of smoke leading the way. Slowly it came towards them in the distance, looking so unearthly and strange.

Love Divine

To the Jewish people this is a description of the people of Israel coming up from the desert on their way to the Promised Land. The Ark of the Covenant carried in the midst of them, moving through the trackless waste of wilderness, led by an unearthly cloud by day and a pillar of fire by night that concealed their God; and all surrounded by mighty warriors armed to protect the Ark that held the religious artefacts of their God. The thousands of people following the cloud and fire at night must have been an overwhelming sight. No wonder the surrounding nations as they watched were filled with awe and fear.

Not only did those who looked upon the hosts of Israel ask the question 'Who is this who comes up from the wilderness?' but the same question was used again and again about the Lord at the beginning of His ministry. People asked, Who was he? Where had He come from?, Who gave him permission to heal and restore the sick? The scribes and Pharisees, the elders and chief priests jeered at the likelihood of a prophet coming from Nazareth, they refused to believe that He was from God and a man 'full of grace and truth.' They were amazed at the words He spoke, His wisdom and the healings and grace He ministered to those around Him. When John the Baptist saw Him he knew that this man who had come to be baptised was the one whom he had been proclaiming; The Man who would lead the people to the true God. When John baptised Jesus, as He rose up out of the River Jordan the Holy Spirit fell upon Him, and God bearing witness from Heaven to His Son spoke, 'Behold the Lamb of God, who takes away the sins of the world.'

John knew this man he was to baptise was the Son of God. Mary the mother of Jesus visited her cousin Elizabeth, the mother of John the Baptist (as recounted in the first chapter of Luke's Gospel, vv 39-56). When Mary greets Elisabeth we're told that the babe in her womb leaped for joy. There is something miraculous happening here; two pregnant women, Elizabeth an older woman, thought to be passed the age of childbearing and Mary, a young virgin. There seems to be another miracle happening. There seems to be some communication between two unborn babies. Elizabeth is humbled to be in the presence of the mother of her Lord. And Mary, rather than exploiting the situation of her own privilege or aggrandisement is moved humbly to worship as the words spoken to her by the angel a few months earlier become even more a reality. The song that we call the Magnificat are the words of God's intention to do great things for his people; that His blessings are available to all in each generation.

The demand and the promise of the Gospel is that the poor should not be exploited by the rich, that the weak should not be oppressed by the powerful; that the proud and wise should come to realise the limits of their wisdom, and those with no privilege be showered with God's graceful gifts.

As we come to believe the truth of that Gospel promise we too leap for joy and humbly are moved to worship. But also we consider how in our lives we are participating in God's Gospel purposes, helping others to find the desire to reach out and touch the things of eternity.

The Magnificat, Mary's acceptance and song to her God:

Love Divine

My soul proclaims the greatness of the Lord, and my spirit rejoices in God my Saviour.

For he has looked with favour on his lowly servant: from this day all generations shall call me blessed.

The Almighty has done great things for me, and holy is his name.

He has mercy on those who fear him in every generation.

He has shown the strength of his arm, he has scattered the proud in their conceit

He has cast down the mighty from their thrones and has lifted up the lowly.

He has filled the hungry with good things, and the rich he has sent empty away.

He has come to the help of his servant Israel, for he has remembered his promise of mercy,

The promise he made to our fathers, to Abraham and his children forever.

Now and down through the ages, hosts of believers answer:

'This is Jesus of Nazareth, the well-loved and only Son of God. This is the Lamb of God who was slain to carry the sins of the world. This is the King of kings, and Lord of lords.'

Verse 6 tells us that as soon as the column was seen, there was the wonderful perfume of myrrh and incense made from all the spices of the merchant carried in the litter. The merchant is a reference to our Lord, and the perfumes and spices refer to the gifts from the Lord. As we consider these spices, which are continually mentioned in the Song, we begin to realise that they reveal to us the nature of Jesus. One inspiring and precious feature of this wilderness journey, is that it is only in the desert that the costly spices and gums are found, and they were used in the Temple during worship and for the embalming of the dead. These spices and gums were found in the deserts of Arabia and the mountains of Palestine. With hard searching and danger merchants found them in the far regions and brought them home. It was an arduous and difficult task either climbing high peaks or descending into deep ravines, but there was great wealth in one cargo of these powders and spices. The bride will only gather these spices and perfumes during her walk in the wilderness of the world. She will not find them in Egypt, or in the heavenly places, but only in the wilderness and during difficult times. The drier and more barren the land, the hotter the testing and harder the paths, the more she will be able to gather this precious cargo to take home to the Lord. The sweetest perfumes are brought out of the hardest suffering and trials. The pure gums come after the tree is pierced, and so with us, only as we are pierced and bruised are the precious attributes of Jesus Christ manifested to the glory of God in us. As the spices are not found in the fertile plains neither are the graces and the fruit of the Spirit perfected in the smooth places in our life, but when we are in the rough hard places. These are usually acquired or given to us when in our ordinary lives we are challenged with difficult relationships, and unforgiving attitudes. Maybe when we are facing the difficulties of jealousy and rejection from others.

Just as the merchants gathered the spices from the arid hot deserts, or hidden deep in the clefts of the steepest mountains and

Love Divine

in other most inaccessible places, it is in our own lives when we are experiencing the most hard difficulties and problems of pain and despair that the Lord Jesus through His love and grace gives us the will to persevere, and trust in Him. And it is often at such times that He begins to change us in the deepest part of our soul, so that eventually we may be changed into His likeness. Humility is the foundation of all the attributes that the Lord wants us to bring to Him. Gathering human love, human humility, human faith and patience must not deceive us, which are only imitations of the heavenly spices and perfumes. These renewing changes that the Lord may bring about in us are all that we will be able to present to our Father in Heaven. As some say, 'There are no pockets in a shroud.' The only things we can offer to God when we enter into heaven are our relationships that we have known on earth, and without any pride we may also pray that God will see the burnishing and depth of the life changing work that the Lord Jesus has created within us.

O Come amongst us mighty Lord.
And grant us grace to do your word,
And in your mercy Lord we pray
Be gentle with us on our judgement day.
For the word of God is living and active,
Sharper than any two edged sword,
it penetrates to even dividing the soul and spirit, joints and
marrow;
It judges the thoughts and attitudes of the heart.
Nothing in all creation is hidden from God's sight.

Everything is uncovered and laid bare before the
eyes of Him to whom we must give account
The Son who dearly purchased you, enfold you
The Father who created you, behold you,
In the friendliness and love of the Holy Trinity.

It was through the seed of David, Jesus was born but His Father was God. It was because of His Humanity that the crowds placed upon Him the crown of thorns and shame. It was the sin of the human race that brought Christ to earth as a man, and to suffer, and wear the crown of thorns.

The chariot that this King made tells us something of the wonder of the King. It is made from the wood of Lebanon, a wood that is so firm and strong that no creature has the strength to burrow into it, and it will never rot. The posts are made of silver, an ore that has to be beaten and melted into shape. In this context it is a symbol of Jesus who although He was the Son of God, was a man like us, and God allowed Him to be tested just as we are. His heavenly Father allowed Jesus to be taken into the desert to face the temptations from the devil: just as we may be tempted. And often after we have been through a difficult 'testing' time we find that God has done some refining work within us. We may not be conscious of that at the time, but later realise that we have reacted to a situation in a better way. Luke tells us that when the Spirit led Jesus into the desert He was *full* of the Holy Spirit, but after He had resisted the temptations of the devil for forty days, as He turned to walk towards Nazareth, He was *filled* with the *power* of the Holy Spirit. The 'man' in Him had passed the test, and so began the ministry of the Lord.

The base of the chariot was pure gold, which in the Bible always speaks of the wonder, power and pure majesty of God. The seat was upholstered in purple, again a very special 'majestic' cloth, (the purple colour is made from the mixture of blue and blood red), and the inside was lovingly inlaid by the daughters of Jerusalem.

The last verse in this chapter speaks of the 'Daughters of Zion' (those who are closest to the King, those who desire to know more of Him, and who want to deepen their lives with Him.) To realise more about His sacrifice, and the crown of thorns, with which humanity crowned Him on the way to the cross, we read that on that day the earth shuddered, mountains were split open and the whole world became dark, and the veil in the temple was torn in two. This signifies to us that this was the day the power that was released and price that was paid for all our sins, so that we can now come into the presence of a Holy God. Not by anything that we may ever do, no matter how great we are, but purely because the Son of God paid that price. Jesus never spoke of himself as the Son of Mary, but as the 'Son of Man'. His Mother was Humanity, for whom He poured out His life.

V.11: Come out you daughters of Zion, and look at the King
wearing the crown,
The crown with which His Mother crowned Him
On the day of His wedding,
The day His heart rejoiced.

'Come out,' says the verse. The words are telling us to come and seek Him. We shall not find Him and see Him by just hoping, living our lives for ourselves and those who are directly connected to us. If we have been shown the reason for the cross, why He had to come to earth, and we begin to understand the crown of thorns that He wore for us, we need to seek Him. If we listen to the voice of God either through friends, the Bible or testimonies of others we need to seek him in this world. The verse tells us that on the day of His wedding His heart rejoiced. He became 'betrothed 'to us on the cross, when He cried out 'It is finished,' He rejoiced because He had achieved all that He came to do.

It is now up to us to find Him on earth and begin to know His wondrous love.

Love Divine

CHAPTER FOUR

V.1: How beautiful you are my love
Oh, how beautiful
Your eyes are doves,
Your hair is like a flock of goats
Descending from Mount Gilead.

From the first four verses in Chapter four we hear the Beloved speaking to the maid. He is telling her how He sees her beauty, but it is not as the world regards beauty. He tells her of the inner beauty that only He knows. He speaks of her features, as we would recognise one another whether we are male or female, but as He describes her, or any soul who is turning towards Him and desiring to follow Him, there is a wonderful depth in the words that He uses. Even if we are feeling unworthy and are aware of our sinful ways and thoughts and attitudes that are not of God, or maybe broken in spirit and in pain because of an unforgiving attitude from others. Or worse feel trapped by an unforgiving heart in our self towards another. He does not abandon us but because of His love and grace He will always stay close to us. He may speak to us of the way that we have disappointed Him. And as we pray asking for forgiveness we will be astounded how the Lord draws us back to Himself.

In Chapter 1 v 15 we have already commented upon the bride's eyes *being* as doves and there are many precious meanings in comparing her eyes *to* a dove. The dove was considered a 'clean' animal and some were set apart to be used as a sacrifice for those who were too poor to bring up a larger animal into the temple worship. After the birth of Jesus, Mary, His mother, because 'her means were not sufficient to offer a lamb' (Leviticus 12 v 8), bought two doves as a sacrifice.

The maid's eyes are fixed upon her Beloved, without any double motive or selfish desires within her. In the Scriptures, the 'eye' is the figure of light and illumination, and as we know the Truth and walk in it, so we shall be purified and see God; 'For only the pure in heart shall see God' (Matthew 5 v 8). I expect everyone has a different picture in their mind of the Lord, according to their nationality and perhaps their age. Except for Daniel's description in the book of Exodus, and the elderly prophet John's description after he was banished to the Isle of Patmos, there appears to be no specific picture of Jesus. They both give wonderful powerful descriptions of the Ancient of Days, referring to God. In the next chapter of this book the maid gives a picture of her Beloved that I always enjoy meditating upon.

V.1: Your hair is like a flock of goats descending from Mount Gilead.

Mount Gilead was shaped like the head and shoulders of a man; and large flocks of goats with long silky hair could be seen grazing and lying down on the steep sides, and so the mountain appeared to be crowned with white hair. In the Bible long hair is seen as the symbol of separation. In both of the Testaments in the Bible there were many who were set apart for God and were seen to be by their long hair. Both the prophet Samuel, and also Samson whom you may remember said that his mighty strength was held in his hair.

V.2: Your teeth are like a flock of sheep just shorn,
coming up from the washing.
Each of them has its twin; not one of them is alone.

A flock of sheep newly shorn are symmetrical and perfect in form Her Beloved is saying that her teeth are perfect and even, without any of them missing or broken, they are also clean without any blemishes. When we remember that food has to be masticated, and prepared by our teeth before it can be swallowed and assimilated to the nourishment of our bodies, we understand the necessity of our teeth, and begin to realise their place in the spiritual health of the bride. Jesus said 'I am the Bread of life, no one comes to the Father except through me.' The more we read about Him in the Bible, worship, pray, and talk to Him, the more we want His life and to follow Him, we begin again to realise that without Him we are nothing. He is our daily bread. Our worldly wealth, or status means nothing, it is our relationship with Him and those around us that really give us peace. We are told to eat of His flesh and drink His blood, during the service of Holy Communion, to literally remember Him and take Him within us. The prophet said: 'Thy words were found, and I did eat them; your words were to me a joy and the rejoicing of my heart; for I am called by your name.' Jesus said: 'I am the bread of life, he who comes to me shall not hunger or thirst'. He is the bread of life, and it is only by faith that we can feed upon Him, it is only by faith that we can drink the water of life. We need to read the Word of God, which becomes nourishing to the whole of the body, it is this faith that guides and draws us to the portion of the Word of God, which when applied will cleanse us.

Some versions of the Bible tells us that it is a 'flock of ewes 'that had come up from the washing, in other words, a flock of female sheep, each of which are twin bearing, and in this way the beautiful flock is increasing and multiplying continually. Every ewe becomes stronger and more beautiful as she feeds upon the grass and drinks from hidden springs. Just as our faith will grow and our knowledge of God will become more intimate as we feed on the word of God in the Bible, we shall learn more about Him, and our lives will become fruitful in His Kingdom. We will start to pray more, and become more aware as we pray and serve others. This verse, even though it speaks of female sheep, of course includes both men and women. We are all in the Christian worldwide Church, as the body of Christ, all who know that they have been forgiven and redeemed by Jesus Christ, and who long to follow His teaching and His ways. All who bear the marks of submission to their unseen Head, will have begun to realise and to know something of His love and peace within themselves, and will also desire to live according to His ways, and desire to know more about Him.

V.3: Your lips are like a scarlet ribbon, your mouth is lovely...

The lips of the bride are like a thread of scarlet, with an open healthy smiling presence. James in his letters to the early church is eloquent and wise in his teaching, inspiring us to be thoughtful with the words that we say. He says, 'Know this, my beloved brethren. Let every man be quick to hear, slow to speak, slow to anger, for the anger of man does not work the righteousness of God'. James was a brother in the family of Jesus, and he did not proclaim the life of his brother until after the resurrection. There must have been many interesting conversations in the family, perhaps sometimes causing pain and misunderstanding. Psalm 141 v 3 says 'Set a watch God, before my mouth, and keep the door of my lips. Let no corrupt speech proceed out of my mouth, but only that which is good for edifying and encouraging to those who have the grace to hear.' The word translated as 'corrupt' literally means 'worthless 'and is taken from a word which means 'to putrefy'. So the final condition of 'worthless words' is described in the original translations as 'putrid'. They are words that have no salt in them, though they may have seemed harmless when spoken. Without grace, (seasoned with salt), words become putrid and 'ill smelling' causing pain and misunderstanding. We do not realise how careless words, when repeated, can be dangerous and hurtful. Even after the person who has spoken words that are unkind and hurtful has died, the person who received them may find it difficult to forgive, and the remembrance of the words may also colour the life of the one to whom they were spoken.

Love Divine

How wonderful it would be for ourselves and those among us if God touched our lips with a live coal from His altar, (Isaiah 6v 6), and forever made our words pure. It is only as our hearts are bound in love to Him, and He pours into them the treasures of His wisdom and grace that we can ever speak the beautiful words that He wishes to hear. 'For out of the fullness of the heart the mouth speaks.'

James tells us that we must be 'quick to hear, slow to speak and slow to anger.' But so often we are quick to speak and teach others, quick to strive and defend ourselves, even when we are in the wrong.

Your temples behind your veil
Are like the halves of pomegranate.

In Scripture the temples or forehead are always spoken of as the seat of boldness or modesty. This comparison to a pomegranate refers to the red and white centre of the fruit after it is cut open; and the seeds are seen to have a red fluid, which combines together with the white pulp. Here it is interpreted as a sign of the modesty of the bride. Her life hidden within Christ. The work must begin within us, as the red of the pomegranate is hidden away inside the rind of the fruit so must our union with the Lord, work within us before it can appear without. It is as we die to self and pride in our heart that the incorruptible hidden life of the Lord grows within us. As we put on Christ within, His humility will appear without; but it is always appears before the face of God before it is seen by man.

118

V.4: Your neck is like the tower of David.
Built with elegance
On it hang a thousand shields, all of them shields of
warriors.

The neck of the bride is like a tower, or fortress that lifts its head high above all regions around it. It is hung with armour, and shields of victory. She walks with elegance and submission as a beautiful bride. She does not walk with her neck bowed down in bondage as she works, and tends the grapes in the vineyards of the world. She knows that she has her place and life *in* the world, but she no longer is *of* the world. Jesus has broken the bondage of sin, and she can walk upright. He has taken away the mark of slavery, and the bondage of law; He has set her free. She is called to this freedom, standing fast in the liberty of the life that she has been called by Jesus. She knows that this new liberty is as a servant to others, but the Lord and His work on the cross of Calvary have broken off every yoke the world and man laid upon her. She knows that she must move with a holy fear and submission to God and His ways, but she is fearless and victorious towards the world, the flesh and the devil. Her neck is like the defensive towers that are hung with armour, it is not proud or wanton, neither stiff-necked nor rebellious, but it is upright, stately and beautiful. When the Lord calls us to Himself and we say that we are sorry for living our lives satisfying our self and our desires, even though we may be all wrapped up in family and friends, we think that if we turn to Him we will lose our liberty. Many think we are free and have liberty but really are bound down and are slaves to the world.

Love Divine

We only have to read of the life of Paul, who rejoiced in calling himself the 'bond slave to the Lord.' He gloried in being the slave of Christ, he rejoiced working as a slave. He longed to be the love slave of his Lord more completely than he had ever been under bondage to his enemies. When we yield to the Holy Spirit within us, and let Jesus release us from every fetter that binds us, and when we choose in all things to serve Him and Him alone He takes away the yokes that have bound us, and in their place He throws over us His yoke of love. His desire is for us to work in the vineyard where we are, where He can trust us, and sometimes we may find that He has led us to achieve things, and to walk along pathways, which we would never ever have dreamt of. In the world sometimes we have to work and spend our life trying to bend our self to the job in hand, but with the Lord He always leads us along a path with a work that fits the body and character that He has given us.

The armour with which we are equipped and through which we will get our victory is described in Ephesians 6 v 10-18:

Finally, be strong in the Lord, and in His mighty power,
Put on the full armour of God, so that you can take your
stand against the devil's schemes,
For our struggle is not against flesh and blood, but against
the rulers, against the authorities, against the powers of the
dark world, and against the spiritual forces of evil in the
heavenly realms.

Therefore put on the full power of God so that when the day of evil comes you may be able to stand your ground, and after you have done everything, to stand.

Stand firm then, with your belt of truth buckled round your waist, with the breastplate of righteousness in place, and with your feet fitted with the readiness that comes from peace.

In addition to all of this, take up the shield of faith, with which you can extinguish all the flaming arrows of the evil one.

Take the helmet of salvation and the sword of the Spirit, which is the word of God.

This is the armour that we all have to protect us during our life on earth, and we must use it to withstand all that may confront us. We must read the Bible and dwell upon the words praying that the Holy Spirit will open up to us all the wisdom and guidance that we need to act upon. 'Let the word of Jesus dwell in you richly.'

God's Word hacks and hews, cuts down and brings to nothing man's ideas in a marvellous way. We must train ourselves not to be concerned as to what man thinks and says, but to be concerned with what God thinks, and what His word declares about all things.

Why is the Bible so incredible? Who compiled it?

We think that 40 different writers wrote it: doctors, scholars, farmers and fishermen, and they wrote their own views on religion, poetry, ethics, science, philosophy, the creation of the universe and where it is going. If you separate these writers and remember that for many the only contact was by word of mouth, and that it was

Love Divine

collected over a period of fifteen hundred years, there is an incredible unity through all the books from Genesis to the book of Revelations. Thus we begin to grasp that it was not just 40 people but one person who wrote it.

Mark Twain said:

It's not the things that I don't understand,
It's the things that I do understand that worry me,
And I am afraid that one day I might meet the Author.

We need to be able to speak to others about our salvation and to be familiar with the real gospel of Jesus Christ and our identification with Him and His death and resurrection. We need to be able to speak about our faith with a certainty that comes from our relationship with Jesus Christ and our willingness to be available for Him on this earth.

V.5: Your two breasts are like two fawns,
Like twin fawns of a gazelle, that browses among the lilies.

The breasts of the maid and the breastplate of the Christian are the same. 1 Thessalonians 5 v 8 tells us 'to put on the breastplate of faith and love.' We know that each one of us begins our walk with Him by faith, and it is impossible to receive anything from God except but by faith. We cannot work up, nor pump up faith; neither can we manufacture it. Our faith and love must begin and grow together If the bride of Christ is going to be perfected, according to this symbolism she must accept her Beloved by faith and recognise His love by the only way possible, putting Him first in her life.

Abraham was called the 'righteousness of God 'because of his faith. It seems incredible to understand such a depth of faith. In about 2615 BC Abraham was living in Ur, the people were descendants of Noah through Shem, (Noah's son) and the people were called Shemarians, or later Sumerians. Ur was the capital of a city-state, which covered the western delta of the Tigris and the Euphrates rivers which flow into what is now known as the Persian Gulf. The land had been drained by a system of canals and dykes and was cultivated with wheat, barley flax, vegetables and orchards of fruit trees; a large part of the civilisation was engaged in farming. There was also a great deal of trade through the port of the gulf bringing in trade, commerce, and special goods through river traffic. With comforts and luxuries provided, a civilisation soon evolved and the citizens of Ur made remarkable advances in accounting and banking, mathematics and astronomy, geology, medicine and literature. Law, justice and all moral standards were kept and honoured. Uniquely, the Tigris Euphrates valley holds vast stores of man's earliest documents inscribed on tablets of clay, these recently discovered libraries are the archives of city states that attained unbelievable advanced civilisations- almost all established between 4500 and 5000 years ago. In all the documents and archives of ancient civilisations, there is little evidence of any systemized paganism. Rather it is being discovered more and more that people in those early times held two strong beliefs. 1) That there is one God- hidden powerful and without a name, and 2) that this same God caused a devastating flood to cover the earth during which only one man and his family were spared. It was not until the third millennium in Ur that a man made his own god, and gave it a shape and a name: -the moon was proclaimed god, the god Nannar-Sin. It was from this city Ur 3000 BC where the insidious sins of paganism incest, drunkenness, and crime were rife. God called Abraham to gather up his family and relatives, to lead them out into the desert, and Abraham obeyed his God. His faith was such that he believed and obeyed, trusting that God would lead him to a promised land: such a tremendous example of faith, and love.

The meaning of the breasts of the bride is beautifully told in Ephesians 3. Paul prays that the Ephesians may be strengthened through the Spirit of God in the inward man; 'that Christ may dwell in their hearts through faith, so that they may be rooted and grounded in love. As we grow in faith and love so we may understand more what is the breadth and length and height and depth, and knowledge of the love of Jesus Christ, that passes all understanding.'

V6: Until the day breaks and the shadows free
I will go down to the mountains of myrrh, and to the hill of
incense.

These words portray the last hours that the Jesus passed with His disciples before the last supper, and just before the crucifixion. Already the lengthening shadows of the approaching night were beginning to fall upon the Lord's time on earth. To the Son of God, these shadows took the form of a rugged cross outside the city walls, as they were with Him right through His childhood. Just as during the day the darkness is dispelled by the sun, so the Sun of Righteousness, who is the Light of the world, dispels the darkness of an evil night. Over and over again the Lord during His last months on earth told His disciples that He must suffer and die. He warned them that the hour of His departure was approaching, but they were unbelieving, not persevering nor hearing that the hour of darkness was approaching and His absence was closing in upon them. Even when they were travelling to Jerusalem and the ignominy and suffering of the cross awaited Him, and the darkness of His absence awaited them, they argued as to who would be the greatest in His kingdom which they thought He was about to set up. For three years He had been with them teaching and talking to them, telling them that 'The Son of Man must suffer many things, and be rejected by the elders and chief priests and scribes and be killed and the third day be raised up,' but they did not hear or comprehend what He was saying. So often we listen but judge things according to our own preconceived ideas.

We too must take notice and discern the times ahead of us, and the Second Coming of the Lord. We must be aware of the times and be mentally prepared for whatever is before us. At all times we must be assured of His continuing presence with us, and remember the prayers that he prayed the night before He was betrayed. This precious farewell from the Son to His Father ends with these wonderful words

Love Divine

*'Righteous Father, though the world does not know you, I
know you,*
*And they (meaning all Christians down the ages) know that
you have sent me.*
*I have made you known to them, and will continue to make
you known in order that the love you have for me, may be in
them, and that I myself will be in them.*[23]

Paul writing to the Romans, having written in the previous
chapters of the book of the wonder and grace of our Lord and the
new life that we can have with Him says in Romans 12 v 1:

Therefore, I urge you, brothers, in view of God's mercy
To offer yourselves as a living sacrifices,
holy and pleasing to God
This is your spiritual act of worship.

Surely our prayer can be no less.

The 'Mountains of Myrrh' is a figure of the tomb in which the
Lord lay until He rose from the dead. 'The Hill of Frankincense'
symbolises the Cross of Calvary, where through the Eternal Spirit
He offered Himself to God. Myrrh reminds us of the preciousness,
the fragrance and the priceless value of Christ and the redemptive
work on the Cross 'Frankincense' is an emblem of His perfect
acceptability before God, and His abandonment to do His will and
glorify Him in all things.

---

[23] John 17 v 20.

In the Garden of Gethsemane, He said 'Father, if it be possible, let this cup pass from me. Nevertheless not my will, but your will be done.'

The purest essences of these perfumes are obtained by piercing the bark of the tree or shrub, and from these wounds flow the resinous gums that are so fragrant and costly. We shall never know until we get to Heaven and Eternity the effect that that these fragrant perfumes of herbs and spices rose to Heaven from the Cross of Calvary and the tomb of our Lord.

'V.7: All beautiful you are my love, there is no flaw in you.

The Beloved has been warning the maid that He must leave, and go to His Father, but He speaks to her tenderly assuring her of His love. He does not go because of any fault in her, or because of lack of love in him in His heart.

Nevertheless I tell you the truth; it is expedient for you that I go away; for if I don't go away the Comforter will not come to you; but if I go away I will send Him to you.[24]

These are words that Jesus used to encourage the disciples, explaining why He was leaving them.

The love of Christ which He expressed so tenderly to those who walked and talked with Him on earth is no further from us today, and just as loving and eternal as He speaks to us, and is within us in this 21st Century. It is this fathomless love of Christ

---

[24] John 16:7, *21st Century King James Version.*

that overwhelms us in a personal way, and it is this boundless love that is the banner that He lifts over us. This verse not only refers to His withdrawal from His disciples when He went to the cross, but also leads us along the same way. Sometimes when our communion is sweetest and we feel that our walk with him has entered into a close intimate relationship and nothing can disturb it, our Beloved suddenly withdraws. Like Job we feel abandoned, if we go forward He is not there, if we turn to the left or right He is not there. He seems indifferent to us and we cannot reach Him. It is then that we must trust Him, and remember that He has not left us, but maybe He wants to teach us a new thing. Whatever is before us He knows, and whatever He does it is for our own sake. He wants us not to just rejoice in His sweetness and love, not because we have entered into a closer relationship with Him, but He wants us to love and rejoice in Him alone.

We must remember that whether seen or unseen, whether felt or unfelt, our Lord is the same yesterday today and forever. His love never changes or never grows cold. James said, 'With Him is no variableness, nor shadow that is cast by turning.' He does not want us to be like Thomas who needed proof. The Lord needs us in a place where we do not have to depend upon our feelings; where, though we do not feel that He is close to us or aware of us, we trust him. He wants us to be so sure of our relationship with him, even though we may feel in darkness and apparent separation, we still remember that His banner is floating over us, and that He can trust us, that we will never waver. We must be as Job who lost everything and lived in 'sackcloth and ashes', but trusted in his

God to the end, and just as Job in the end of his life gained more riches than he ever had experienced before, so shall we as we enter Eternity receive all that God has for us. The best is yet to be..

As I write this I remember again those today who are persecuted, who lose everything even their families and livelihood, but still in spite of every hardship remain strong in their faith.

Maybe we should echo this prayer in our hearts:

Power of God, protect us, Love of God lead us
Spirit of God strengthen us, In all life and all creation.

It is symbolic that in verse 8 the Beloved is calling to His bride,

Come with me from Lebanon my bride,
Come with me from Lebanon
Descend from the crest of Anana, from the top of Senir the
summit of Hermon,
the lions' dens and the mountain haunts of the leopards.

Lebanon was a border mountain between enemy country and the Promised Land, and the Hebrews never conquered it. It is symbolic of the spiritual borderland between the world and Heaven; between compromise and fidelity to God; between half-heartedness and abandonment to God. These border lands were infested with lions and leopards lurking in the hiding places and the clefts of the rocks, ready to spring out to any belated traveller. They were filled with dangers from deep chasms and precipices.

Love Divine

The lion is a symbol of open foe ready to devour any unsuspecting creature, and is full of hatred towards anyone open to God. The leopard is a symbol of the enemy as a subtle, fierce swift foe enraged against mankind. In the book of Revelations 13 v 2 the leopard is used as an emblem of the Antichrist. It is in the borderlands that the enemy is on the prowl ready to capture and destroy those who are seeking to escape from the corruption that reins in the world from lust and covetousness.

The enemy does not pursue and attack those who are in the world and have no desire to seek God, nor does he attack those who are secure in their knowledge of God through Jesus Christ. It is those who linger between the world and the Church of Christ that the enemy directs his efforts. In the natural world once we have crossed a mountain we do not have to face it again, but spiritually, the mountains of decision, which lie between God's best and compromise in us, are continually facing us in our path with Him. Each day every one of us has decisions to solve, people with whom we relate and love and care for, good things and not so easy problems facing us. Once you have by faith planted your life in God's Kingdom, it will not be 'roses all the way', but you will have the assurance that He is always with you, and His desire is for the best for you.

The Beloved of the maid does not want her to loiter in the ways of indecision, and uncertainty. He wants her to possess all that He has bought for her. He has brought her out of the kingdom of darkness into the kingdom of light, and He does not want her to be in the questionable regions that separate light from dark

V.9: You have stolen my heart, my sister my bride,
You have stolen my heart with one glance of your eyes,
With one jewel of your necklace.

When we read these words from the Beloved as He encourages her, we cannot but think of the Lord when He looked upon His mother and family, upon His disciples and all those who followed Him and loved Him during His time on earth. How he must have loved those who had believed in Him, those who had followed Him and would soon suffer for Him, during His last days on earth. He knew that He was walking towards the cross, and they would soon be bereft not really understanding why it had to be. He foresaw their distress when the soldiers surrounded Him and took Him away, and when He was condemned in the judgement hall, when He was scourged and spat upon and had to carry His own cross. He saw their grief and perplexity when He was nailed upon the cross and as they stood and watched Him hanging there. But He knew that after their night of fear and sorrow there joy would be full in the morning. With the dawning of these days of Grace they would see Him raised from the dead, and for a short time He would be with them until He ascended into Heaven, by which time they were assured of their faith and soon would be filled with His Holy Spirit. These words of love from the Beloved as she glances towards Him during His trial and what seemed like utter defeat to those who had followed Him must have comforted Him. Jesus Christ was the Son of God, but He also was fully man, and would feel the extraordinary pain of hanging on the cross, and the utter abandonment and humiliation from those about him.

131

Love Divine

I can tell you of a story when a little girl of six must have stolen the eyes of Jesus as she turned to Him. She now is a wife and mother of three little children living in Scotland. When she was in her first primary school in small Scottish town, the nurse had found a little girl with nits in her hair. At playtime all the class turned to kick and shout at the unfortunate little girl, but because this other little girl would not join in with them, they turned on her too. She ran away to the corner of the playground, and asked Jesus what she should do. Just then the bell rang; it was time for home and the weekend.

She was still crying when she met her Mother, who very sensibly said, 'Well, you asked Jesus, and He will give you the answer before school on Monday.' I am sure her parents added their prayers to the situation, and on the Sunday evening she quietly told her Mother that she thought would write a letter and say that she would be the friend of this unfortunate six year old, and give it to her friend before they went into school.

V.10: How delightful is your love, my sister my bride,
How much more pleasing is your love that wine,
And the fragrance of your perfume than any spice.

These words in the Song can make us feel so unworthy of such love from the Lord, Whatever we may be experiencing, or however we feel, we know that we would be as nothing without His love and the work on the cross. It is difficult to believe that we in our puny lives can ever be a delight to the Lord, even to the extent that He says one glance of our eyes to Him is worth more than any of

132

the riches on earth, even to the gifts of oil and costly spices. If we remember that in Chapter 1, the maid already has begun to realise that her Beloved's love 'is as oil poured out', in other words completely and utterly unselfish becoming as nothing Himself because His love for her is so great, and yet He says that her love means everything to Him. As we ponder over these verses surely they cause us to turn towards Him. For some this means the loss of friends and reputation, for some persecution for His Name's sake because of the devoted love and loyalty of men and women. Always our love grows even more deeply, as we experience and understand more of the pain of the cross.

A sacramental prayer:

Now let us from this table rise,
renewed in body mind and soul;
With Christ we die, and live again,
His selfless love has made us whole.[25]

---

[25] Quoted from a hymn by Fred Kaan, b.1929.

Love Divine

V11 'Your love drops sweetness as the honeycomb, my bride,

Milk and honey are under your tongue,

The fragrance of your garments is like that of Lebanon.

Milk and honey represent nourishment and edification. It is as we feed upon the sincere milk of the Word that it is stored away in our hearts, and honey is found under our tongues.

How can we become so that our lips and our love can speak without bitterness and deceit wherever we are, and to anyone to whom we are speaking, and so bring to the Beloved the joy and sweetness of a heart that is totally at one with Him? The only way in which the lips and tongue can be cleansed is by the Holy Spirit of God working within us. When the living Word of God is lodged deep in our hearts any bitterness is changed to honey, and poisonous thoughts are changed into milk. It is by the grace of God. We cannot earn it, count it or store it. The 17th century Thomas Traherne said that 'When he went to Oxford 1653 he found that his tutors were indeed very learned, but they taught their subjects as things unrelated to each other, as technical knowledge and not with the wisdom necessary for true human flourishing.' In our human condition 'we were made to love as the sun is to shine' yet the flawed love and ways that we conduct ourselves which we all know and experience leaves us with an unholy imprint on us. The only way we can be restored is through the love of Christ who 'emptied himself 'poured himself out, taking our human nature upon Himself, all our sin, covetousness, arrogance, and hatred for one another by paying the price for us on the cross. The cross of

Christ which we see with His hands outstretched in the gesture of human love yet pinned by nails to rough wood, and mocked and spat upon as a slashed victim of a heinous murder, shows the nature of that Divine love which gives to the uttermost. Austen Farrer once said, 'Grace flows like sunlight from God to us, and can no more be stored than sunlight can be stored. Yet you must turn your face to the rays to receive that Grace.'

At a deeper level than that which any science can prove, Christ feeds in us the Grace of Himself. Nothing comes from the outside, and when we act from the resources of Grace that He gives us, the Holy Spirit within us, feeds the deep root of our will and changes our self and the actions that we say and do. No other way can we speak and live our lives as 'the sweetness of the honeycomb' for the Lord.

The verse ends with 'The fragrance of your garments is like that of Lebanon.'

We are told to put on Jesus Christ; and as He becomes our garment, as He clothes us more and more so His life will become more perceptible in us. Many women worldwide use perfumes, oil and spices so that the air surrounding them is fragrant, often bringing to mind special places that have given pleasure. Our life and walk and carriage, our manner of speech, the least movement in our lives should be permeated with the special spiritual grace and presence, even as the Song says as 'the trees of Lebanon are known by their fragrant perfume.'

Mother Theresa (1910-1997) was a Catholic nun from Albania who had Indian Citizenship, and who founded the Missionaries of

Love Divine

Charity in Calcutta in 1950. For 45 years she ministered to the poor, the sick, orphaned and dying and by the time she died there were 450 centres of Charity around the world, with 4,000 sisters and an associated brotherhood with 300 members. The mission had 610 centres in 23 countries. She and her missionary nuns were easily recognised in their white saris with deep blue borders quietly 'helping the poorest amongst the poor.' A symbol of hope to many, the aged, the destitute, the unemployed the diseased and those abandoned by their families. Mother Theresa was known to say, 'All I need are two saris and a bucket'. She brought peace and prayer to all those in need, some of whom were literally left to die in the streets. I am told that when she was invited to the B.B.C and was gently guided along the corridor towards her appointment, doors kept quietly opening along the corridor by everyone who wanted to see this amazing nun. Such a thing had never happened before for any Royalty, politician or distinguished person, but everyone wanted to observe this small lady in her white sari, with her quiet serene presence, a true woman of God.

Speaking of a saint like Mother Theresa reminds me of Martin Luther in 16th Century when he described Jesus saying:

He ate, he drank, he slept and walked,
He was weary, sorrowful rejoicing
He wept, he laughed
He knew hunger and thirst and sweat
He talked , he toiled he prayed

So there was no difference between him and other men
Except He was God, and had no sin.

V. 12: You are a garden locked up, my sister my bride;
You are a spring enclosed, a sealed fountain.
Your plants are an orchard of pomegranates with choice
fruits,
With henna and nard, nard and saffron
Calamus and cinnamon, with every kind of incense tree
With myrrh and aloes and all the finest spices.

The Beloved has been calling the maid to leave any doubtful thoughts of her previous life and ways, and encourages her by describing how He sees her.

He calls her to remember the gardens prepared for her. God placed Adam in the Garden of Eden, a place of light and beauty, where there was 'every tree that is pleasant to the sight, and good for food.' It was in this garden that mankind fell to the tempter, dragging the whole human race down with him into sin and death.

It was in a garden, overshadowed by a darkness that covered the whole land, and amid the quaking of the earth, and the splitting and pushing up of huge mountains, that Jesus Christ, the second Adam, died.

It was at that moment that the tombs opened up, from which many of the saints arose who had fallen asleep. He brought up with Him out of spiritual death all who would believe upon His name throughout all the ages; and He gave them everlasting life. Death came from the first Adam in the Garden of Eden, and eternal life came through the second Adam in the Garden of the tomb.

In order to open the way into the great Garden of the Kingdom of God our Lord passed through two gardens. The first was the garden of Gethsemane, which led to the cross, and the second was the tomb in which a rich man Joseph from Arimathea a disciple of Jesus had built for himself. He asked Pilate if he could take the body to bury it. He carefully wrapped it in clean linen, and gently laid it in his new tomb, which he had hewn out of the rock. Then he rolled an enormous stone at the entrance. It was in that garden Jesus finished the work, which would open the Kingdom of Heaven to all who would believe upon His name. After three days He rose again and was seen by over 550 people, on 11 separate occasions over a period of 6 months, proving to the world that He was who He said He was and He had accomplished on earth what He came to do.

No one on earth can ever understand the agony and suffering the Lord encountered as, alone with God His Father, He agonized until sweat as great drops of blood fell to the ground. Alone He passed through those hours of agony, while His disciples slept a short distance away. How many of us grow tired and weary, or are taken up with self, and become indifferent to our faith and are drifting away from the truth. Few of us are willing to suffer the reproach of the cross, and the cost of the truth of the pure Gospel except those who are killed and persecuted for their faith in many countries today.

It was in this garden of Gethsemane that the Lord chose that the will of God should be accomplished.

He prayed 'My Father, if it is possible, let this cup pass from me; nevertheless, not as I will, but according to your will it shall be done.' We sometimes think that because He came to die, there was no choice presented to Him after He came on earth. It is unmistakable that there was a choice, and that it was made with great suffering and agony. So often we forget that He was not only the Son of God but also was fully man, and so He would experience all the pain that this most terrible cruel death brought about.

The second garden through which the Lord passed was the garden where He was crucified, and where He was buried; the hill of frankincense and the mountain of myrrh.

A spring enclosed a sealed fountain.

Jesus was the great fountain of life, but was closed to humanity until it was opened at His death, when He was raised from the dead. All men were under the sentence of death, and He died that the sentence might be removed, and we all might have life more abundantly. When He cried, 'It is finished,' as He died upon the cross at Calvary that this Eternal Fountain was opened.

Jesus Christ was the fountain sealed. His tomb was sealed by the Romans at the request of the Jews, because Jesus had foretold His resurrection on the third day. For three days the Fountain of all life was sealed in the tomb not by the Roman seal but by the foreordained plan of Go: 'As Jonah was three days and three nights

Love Divine

in the belly of the whale, so shall the Son of Man be three days and three nights in the heart of the earth. '

To many this Fountain of life will remain sealed; those who resist the drawing of God, and who resist Jesus Christ the fountain will remain sealed. However none of us really know why some remain outside the Kingdom that Jesus came to reveal and offer to us. Only God knows the silent prayers that are whispered as this life comes to an end.

Each one of us as we become a 'Garden enclosed to the Lord, whose wish is to be separated to Him so that He may be glorified' will be drawn closer to the Vine, Christ is the true Vine, and we are the branches, and it is through the branches He bears fruit; and the world judges Christ by the fruit in our lives. If there are fruits of bitterness, untruthfulness, self-righteousness then He is dishonoured. It is as we are called and we respond to work in the Garden He will then anoint us:

> *...to.preach good news to the poor, to bind up the broken hearted,...to proclaim freedom from the captives,...and release from darkness the prisoners...to comfort all who mourn...and those who grieve in Zion, and bestow on them a crown of beauty instead of ashes....a garment of praise instead of despair. They will be called oaks of righteousness, a planting of the Lord for their display of splendour.* [26]

---

[26] Isaiah 61,v1-3.; 4v 13-15

140

These are the words that Isaiah prophesied explaining to the people the work that the coming Messiah would achieve on earth, and which the young man Jesus read aloud in the Temple proclaiming that this is the work that He had come on the earth to achieve. This is the work that the Lord will enable His children to minister to others through the enabling of the Holy Spirit and furthering His Kingdom on earth.

Vv.13-15: Your plants are an orchard of pomegranates with choice fruits,
With henna and nard, nard and saffron, calamus and cinnamon.
And every kind of incense tree, with myrrh and aloes and all the finest spices.
You are a garden fountain, a well of flowing water streaming down from Lebanon.

From small tender shoots grow these orchards and precious fruits, which flow from Christ's life flowing within us. The pomegranate is a symbol of fruitfulness; and of all the fruit that comes from Christ living out His life within us, His precious eternal fruit.

Closely connected with Christ's life, death and burial are the costly fragrant spices. Much is mentioned of the perfumes and spices. The anointing He received and the fragrant oils and spices from the hands of the women who loved Him with a surpassing love while He was on the earth seem to be more precious to Him than all that was done for Him. The odour of the costly spikenard

Love Divine

with which Mary from Bethany anointed Him, filled the whole house, and no doubt, remained with Him until He lay in the tomb, because the perfume from those rare precious oils was most penetrating and lingered for many weeks.

V.15: You are a garden fountain, a well of living water streaming down from Lebanon.

The mountain of Lebanon was always covered with a crown of snow, and the streams of pure cold water flowed down its sides or found its way through underground channels to the thirsty valleys below. These mountain streams never failed, never became stale and tasteless, warm and unrefreshing. From a higher source. than an earthly mountain comes the living water with which we are refreshed; though the Channel through which it flowed, appeared so lowly when upon earth.

Jesus Christ is the Fountain of all gardens and vineyards in the Kingdom of God, and we must receive all our refreshment from Him and Him alone. No matter how fierce the wind may blow, nor how hot the valley is through which we are passing, if we keep the connection open between our souls and the great Fountain of life, the Well of living streams will never dry up but will flow throughout our lives from the Living God.

V.16: Awake, north wind, and come south wind!
Blow on my garden that its fragrance may spread abroad.

Jesus spoke to Nicodemus, a member of the Jewish council who had come to talk to Jesus in the night because of fear of the rest of his fellow Rabbi's. He wanted to find out how this man Jesus could perform the miracles and signs unless God was with Him. Jesus told him that no one could see the Kingdom of God unless he was born again. He told this Pharisee 'I tell you the truth that no man can enter the Kingdom of God unless he is born of water and the Spirit. Flesh gives birth to flesh, but the Spirit gives birth to the spirit. Jesus then went on to say 'You must be born again, the wind blows where ever it pleases, you hear its sound but you cannot know where it comes from or where it is going. For God so loved the world that He gave His one and only Son that whoever believes in him shall not perish but have eternal life. For God did not send His Son to condemn the world, but to save the world through Him.'

The word, 'wind', in both the Hebrew and in the Greek, is the same word that is translated 'spirit'

In John 3 v 8 the word translated 'wind', is the same Greek word that is translated 'Spirit' in other places. The disciple John tells us in Ch. 14 that the way into the Kingdom of heaven was opened through the advent of Christ and His death. Jesus spoke to the disciples encouraging them that when He left them, they would not be alone. He would not leave them desolate or orphans, but would pray to the Father so that they would have another Comforter, the Holy Spirit, whom the world could not receive.

143

Love Divine

In this verse the maid is calling upon the Holy Spirit to perfect in her His work in her life even if it maybe the harsh cold wind of the north. He is the Spirit of truth and He may reveal in us our plans and desires for our self, our own interests, our likes and dislikes, our experiences and self absorption, which eat out the strength and life of our relationship with the Lord. Can we say 'Awake O north wind and blow into the garden of my life?' She is saying, ' Lord send down the tests and trials that you see I need. I want the blossom in my life to bear fruit and stand the test for you.' How many of us having received a revelation of God and heard His call, even rejoiced in Him, but have not yielded to His gentle ways of strengthening. Sometimes in a garden a fruit tree that was wonderful and full of colour in the Spring, when the autumn comes there are just a few mangy specimens of fruit, instead of the rich fruit of former years.

If the Lord just sent the Spirit as a warm south wind with its balmy soft breathings to blow upon us, instead of the sharp blasts of dealing and conviction by the Holy Spirit, so often the real life and possibilities within us would be choked by self esteem and false hopes. The love that suffers all things and is kind must be tried in the furnace before it turns to gold. Our love towards God and towards man maybe tried to the uttermost through suffering, but the divine work that is accomplished within us we pray will never leave us, and we thank God that through it all we know more of Him through the trial.

We may not experience the hardships and trials that many Christians do in countries like North Korea, Iran, Afghanistan, Saudi Arabia, Somalia, Yemen and Iraq to name but a few.

We can pray for those who are threatened for loving the name of Jesus, for protection for them from evil, and help them so that they might bring your glory to others. 'Show them your strength Lord, in the power of your Holy Spirit and draw them closer to yourself, O Lord.

'Lord we pray for your Heavenly Spirit for all the women who suffer oppression and grief. Give them your courage Lord and provide for them daily. Show them your strength, and I pray that you will draw them ever more close to yourself, and that they may experience your love for themselves to give them the strength to build up and care for the broken hearted.

'Lord we pray from the bottom of our hearts for all the young and little children who are deprived of love joy and peace. Guard them and save them and Lord we pray that you will bring healing in all their memories and that you will be their strength and hope in the future.'

Amen.

V.16: Let my Beloved come into His garden and eat his choicest fruits.

This clause applies to the Last Supper our Lord ate with His disciples. Sometimes we may find it difficult to comprehend that no one, not even the disciples had any insight into the particular significance of this spiritual festival of the Passover lamb that they

Love Divine

were commemorating and eating. The Lamb was actually sitting with them. He who was the Sacrifice to which all other sacrifices pointed, the only Sacrifice that would avail for the sin of the world, was sitting with them. He, the Lamb of God, whom the Passover prefigured, ate the Passover with the disciples, but they did not comprehend the significance, nor realise the great change that was about to take place.

The garden is His garden and does not belong to the bride. All the precious fruits are for Him. Every fruit that is perfected in her life is for Him, and is perfected by Him. Though they are perfected in her life and sometimes spoken of as hers, they are really His; because He has given them to her and perfected them within her, and her union with Him in all that she does.

CHAPTER FIVE

V.1: I have come into my garden my sister, my bride
I have gathered my myrrh with my spice
I have eaten my honeycomb with my honey;
I have drunk my wine and my milk.

The garden to which the Lord has come is the garden of spices. Everything in it is mature, the spices and seeds from the fruit have ripened, the honeycomb has produced its honey and the grapes have been gathered and distilled. It is symbolic of the finished work of the cross after the 33 years that the Lord was on the earth, and the fulfilling of all that He came to do in obedience to His Father. The highest archangel could not redeem man, nor could God redeem man except by Jesus, His Son. He became a man so that He could die for all sinners, and took the form of a servant so that He could redeem humanity and that those He redeemed might become His bride. We ourselves must be transfigured into the likeness of Christ, as fellow heirs, which can only be done as we put on Christ through His work as we produce the crops, in His garden, and our union with Him in that work. The Lord knew that the Passover supper He took with the disciples was the last time that He would eat with them, even though they were not aware that the Lamb (Jesus) was about to be slain. After they had eaten Jesus broke bread which He shared with the disciples, and then He filled His glass of wine which He passed round to them all, and so He instituted the betrothal supper, or the act of

Love Divine

Communion with Him, and which as we take part, reminds us of His cross and our union with Him. He wanted to convey to the disciples what was before Him, that He was to be broken and His blood spilt after they arrived in Jerusalem.

V.1: I have gathered my myrrh with my spice; I have eaten my honeycomb and honey;
I have drunk my wine and my milk.

While the Lord was on earth He gathered all the myrrh and spices. In John's Gospel Chapter 17 in his prayer before He went to the cross Jesus tells His Father:

I have accomplished the work which you gave me to do
Those you gave me I have kept. Now they know that
everything you have given me, has come from you.
For I gave them the words that you gave me, and they have
accepted them.
I have given them your word, and the world has hated them
for they are not of this world
My prayer is not that you take them out of the world, but
that you protect them
Sanctify them by the truth; your word in us the truth.

This priestly prayer from Jesus, and the persecution and hate that He received during His three years speak of the volumes of the herbs and spices that the Lord gathered in His Garden. Even the

Lord's brothers did not believe in Him, and today still many are mocked and jeered at, even killed for their belief in Jesus Christ.

Isaiah 53 tells us:

He grew up before him like a tender shoot, and like a root
out of dry ground.
He had no beauty or majesty to attract us to Him.
He was despised and rejected by men,
A man of sorrows and familiar with suffering
Like one from whom men hide their faces,
he was despise and rejected and we esteemed him not.

It was not easy for Him to come to earth and gather His myrrh and spices. He came and drank the cup of God's wrath, so that our cup might be mingled with God's mercy.

I have drunk my wine and my milk.

In those days the first food given to a baby was to have their lips wetted with the juice of a grape to make them 'suck in' and begin to breathe, and then they were given honey, the complete food from the comb, before they were put to the breast for milk.

Honey was also a symbol of the word of God. To feed upon God's word, is to yield to God so that His Word and the gospel become food to us as it is daily lived in our lives. It was when Jesus yielded to the will and plan of God, becoming a man, so that He could redeem us, that He ate His honeycomb and honey.

Love Divine

What was the cup to which Jesus referred when He asked the disciples if they were able to drink the cup that He was about to drink? It was this cup referred to in the Song of Solomon, the cup of the wrath of God. He drank it so that you and I need not drink it. If He had not drunk that cup we would have to drink it; we would have God's face turned away from us, and would be banished for ever from His presence.

Though we take with Him this cup in death to sin and self, it is not the same bitter cup that He drank, but it is entering into the death, which He has already provided. Through His life, there may be suffering, but in us He can bring peace and even joy for those who love Him.

How little we really go through pain and injustice to drink the cup that He holds out to us, for God prepared the works that we should walk in them. Ephesians 2 v 10 says:

For we are God's workmanship, created in Jesus Christ to
do good works,
which God prepared in advance for us to do.

When we are going through difficult times, which we all have to face, we need to continually remember that the Lord knows all that is happening, and anything we might encounter is only a infinitesimal speck compared to all He suffered for us. So many times instead of gathering myrrh, frankincense and wonderful spices we gather wormwood or bitter roots, and instead of gathering honey we gather thistles and thorns. When we should be gathering the spikenard of humility, we are gathering the vile smelling weeds of pride; instead of gathering the precious attributes that He will give us to enable us and strengthen us. We hold on to the weeds of our own flesh and our own desires, instead of receiving the fragrant oils of the fruits of the Holy Spirit, and the gifts that the Lord wants to give us to enable us to achieve the life that He has for us. We can only take to heaven that which the Lord has wrought within us.

V.2: I slept but my heart was awake,
Listen, my Beloved is knocking;
'Open to me, my sister my bride,
My dove, my flawless one.
My head is drenched with dew
My hair with the dampness of the night.

The scene is changing as time moves on from the Last Supper. The shadows were already beginning to fall although the disciples did not discern them; they were the harbinger of the awful darkness that was about to cover the earth as the King of Glory died. They had eaten the last Passover they would ever eat with Him; they had taken the first 'Communion' or Sacrament, which would become the Service of Remembrance the world over.

I slept but my heart was awake.

Historically this is speaking of the disciples who loved Him and gave their lives to follow Him, but who slept while He was

Love Divine

agonizing in the garden, and whose hearts were not open to the words He spoke.

I wonder if we would behave as the Bride. She is half awake because she does not want to miss the Lord speaking to her, but she wants to rest and take her ease. When a soul is following the Lord, those around her may recognise that she does hear His voice, but are comforted that in their eyes she is not fanatical or overzealous and will happily take her ease. Neither the world nor backslidden Christians like to see too much zeal, which they always call fanaticism.

We know that the bride did not go into the sin of infidelity, for He called her His love, His dove, His undefiled. His love was upon her, and her love was towards Him but she had become tired and despondent. She had washed her feet, she had prepared for bed and laid down on her couch with the express purpose of sleep and rest, but she did not want the sleep to be so deep that she would not hear her Beloved's voice. The Lord had called her to a place of a more intimate communion with Him, He wants her to be willing to enter into a walk with Him which she would find at the foot of the cross. How many times we hear the voice of the Lord and are thrilled that He is calling us to a higher ground, but we stop and consider should we leave our place of ease, should we lose the admiration and influence that we have on others because they know we hear and are 'religious'. Are we willing to follow Him and trust Him where ever He leads us? We may be in a place to hear and know the voice of the Lord and yet not follow after Him hard enough to convict anyone. We love Him; we are not backslidden into sin, only into indolence, and love of ease and the admiration of others. It is comforting and pleasing to be in this place of half slumber, but we are not obedient, we are not counting all things but loss for the excellence of the knowledge of Jesus Christ the Lord.

V.3: I have taken off my robe- must I put it on again?
I have washed my feet must I soil them again?

Is this the maid who ran after Him with such speed that her Beloved likened her to one of the horses in Pharaoh's chariot? Is this she who ran through the city streets seeking Him her soul loved?

Is this she who when she had found Him, clung to Him with such abandonment and would not let Him go?

Is this she who has just sat with Him at the betrothal supper and has gone with Him into the garden of spices?

Is this the bride of the Lamb who is answering the voice and the knock of her Beloved, as she would answer a stranger who was asking for shelter?

She does not realise what it means not to open the door to Him, just because she feels drowsy.

What trifles have we put before God when He has knocked at our door calling us to a higher ground? The devil will always suggest something that we can do for our Lord or for His children, which will soothe our consciences when we do not obey His voice. We so often do not realise that He is calling us to be in a place where He can do something for us. The bride loses what God is

Love Divine

offering her and misses the blessing and revelation that He is waiting to bring her.

The best God has for her she lets slip through her powerless fingers.

Vv.4-5: My Beloved thrust His hand through the latch opening,
My heart began to pound for Him.
I arose to open to my Beloved, and my hands dripped with myrrh,
My fingers with dripping myrrh, on the handles of the lock.

Her Beloved has called and knocked but she has not listened or risen to open the door. So he tries to open it Himself, and finds that she has not only closed the door but locked it. In those days they used a device for fastening the door, which could be managed from inside or outside through a hole in the door made for this purpose. Her Beloved finds that she has locked it from the inside. The Bridegroom could have broken open the door and entered in, just as He could break open the doors of our hearts and enter, but He never does. He calls us, and encourages us, He knocks through His goodness and kindness; but when we refuse to open He will stretch out His hand and gently chasten us. Much of the correction and chastening through which we have passed would not be necessary if we had listened to the voice of our Lord. If the bride had opened the door at once, her Beloved would have come in and she would not have wandered the streets; she would have escaped the humiliation she suffered from others as she went about the streets. Many of us have passed through experiences that have seemed to be unbearable at the time, because in no other way could He give us that which He had for us.

Many years ago I suffered from a terrible depression, which my doctor told me that if I had a cancer of the breast he would be more optimistic that I would be cured. I had reached the stage of wanting to go into a mental home rather than face the world. Fortunately a leader of the church suggested that I should pray with a minister and his wife. During the first session of prayer the Holy Spirit reminded me of many occurrences that had happened to me in the past. After the first session, as I drove home through the beautiful county of Yorkshire I had to stop the car, I had begun to feel as though I was covered in a beautiful cloth of gold. I wandered what was happening and then I realised that the Lord was confirming that the ministry I was receiving was in His will. I had to receive this ministry several times as the Holy Spirit brought to my mind injustices and mental cruelty I had received as a child. After I had been led to forgive those who had caused these times in my life, I was healed and the depression vanished. Since then I have at times thanked the Lord for the whole experience, and all of the past and His healing, because I know that He can heal a deep depression, and as I have prayed with others He has again healed their hurts and pain. None of us will ever experience a tiny dot compared to the pain of the cross.

During this time I was in full-time ministry in the church. However, several years later I had to go through a dreadful experience of rejection, and I knew I would not have survived if the Lord had not taken me through this path of inner healing. Maybe He had been trying to cause me to open my heart during the preceding years and I just continued with what I thought was more important, but I praise Him that He persevered, and eventually led me along a path of ministry I would never have been fit for or achieved.

We are His hands and feet in this world. If we turn to Him, and want to honour Him with our lives, then we need to listen and respond to whatever He asks. There is nothing equal to the resignation (even if we have been slow to respond) and the humility that leads to obedience, and to self-effacement.

V.6: I opened for my Beloved
But my Beloved had left, He was gone,
My heart sank at His departure, I looked for Him
But did not find Him, I called Him but He did not answer.

Even when the maid does eventually open up the door she does not expect that He will have withdrawn; this thought had not come to her. How many times it is so with us, we loiter, are indifferent, take our time, not caring whether we hurry or are obedient straight away. We praise our Lord for His patience and love, but He will not always be there waiting. He is our Lord and we must trust Him, and ask for forgiveness when we tarry.

The myrrh on the bride's hands is an emblem of the anointing and dealing of the Holy Spirit, together with the deep repentance, which always follows after His dealings with us. The liquid myrrh which is gathered after the bark has been cut, is most precious, and

156

is a figure of abandonment to the Holy Spirit that comes from humbling one's self and repentance, and is shown in prayer and praise, love and humility, poured out to Jesus.

I opened the door.

Jesus never forces any door open; He only comes in when we have opened the door. There is no power in hell or on earth that can prevent us getting all that God has for us, but only one person can open the door.

V.6: But my Beloved had withdrawn Himself and had gone.
My heart sank at his departure
I looked for him but did not find Him
I called but He did not answer.

As soon as she is aroused, He passes on; and she begins to realise what she has done. She looks out into the darkness, out into the night, which seems so much darker than if she had been with her Beloved. The fact that He is not there is an incentive to seek after Him more diligently. If the Lord never tested us, we would be slow to mature, and slow to learn to hear Him. The more He has given us, the more He has worked with us, the more He can trust us to seek Him and after we are once convicted and awakened, there is nothing that will more subtly steal away that which the Lord is offering us, than a spirit of procrastination and laziness.

Little does she care now whether she soils her feet, nor does she care about the comfortable bed of ease she was enjoying or what it would cost to find her Beloved. She runs out into the dark city streets to find Him.

V.7: The watchman found me as they made their rounds in
the city
They beat me, they bruised me;
They took away my cloak, those watchmen of the city walls.

The words 'watchman', 'shepherds' 'keepers of the city walls' all have the same meaning; they are the pastors and teachers whom the Chief Shepherd has made over the sheep. There is another historical meaning to these words. It was not the Romans who came to seize Jesus, it was 'a multitude with swords and staves from the chief priests and the scribes and elders,' or in other words, 'From the watchman in Israel and the keepers of the walls.' They were not like the elders in the third chapter whom she had met in her longing for the Lord and who led her along the way and taught her. These are watchmen who have become jealous of her love for the one her soul loves, and no doubt feel guilty that they have lost their first love for the Lord. They make no effort to help her; instead they bruised her and took away her cloak. No greater indignity can come upon an oriental woman than to have her veil removed. In those days, and even now in some countries, it is only women of ill repute who go unveiled.

If we read an autobiography or know any particular saint today there always seems to be a time of persecution and difficulties. It is as if the persecution and difficulties that they endured hones and deepens their knowledge and love of God. The

Lord does not persecute us, but He will allow certain things to happen to us, and then anoints us and teaches us through them.

V.8: O daughters of Jerusalem I charge you-
If you find my Beloved, what will you tell him?
Tell Him I am faint with love.

Although this is similar to her appeal to the daughters of Jerusalem in the second chapter it is not the same. Now there is a touching humility with which she assumes that it is possible for them to find Him, for now she is sick with love, because of His absence and her love and longing for Him. Her love and abandonment have increased, being stirred by the contrition, which her neglect of the Lord has aroused in her. Though absent, He is more real and she longs for Him more than ever before. There is quite a hint of desolation in this cry from the maid. Her indolence and love of self has blighted her confidence and assurance, and she fears that she might not find Him again.

When we think of Advent we remember the weeks before Christmas and we look forward to celebrating the birth of Jesus. Sometimes it is helpful to look back on our own lives in our walk with Jesus Christ and see that we are living a continual advent with Him. If we look back to our first calling and our first confrontation with Him when we may have made a life commitment to Him and He began to draw us towards His love. Often when we look back we see that many times, possibly more often than not, there have been difficulties and problems. As we recollect we begin to see that it has been particularly at such times our faith and love have grown. We realise that along the way He has been continually teaching us and strengthening us, so that we can be honed to become a little more like Him and entrusted with the fruits and gifts of the Spirit. It is as we become mature Christians in the Body of Christ we see that He has opened pathways for us, far more than we could ever have imagined.

V.9: How is your Beloved better than others,
most beautiful of women?
How is your Beloved better than others, that you charge us
so?

These are again the friends of the maid. They become aware of the unconscious humility and consuming hunger of one who has a deep relationship and experience with the Lord. When a deep devotion is seen and lived, others may be aroused and begin to seek out such love for themselves.

Those in our homes know how close we are walking with Him; those who are touching our lives also know whether we really have a hunger for Him, whether we are really humble towards others or whether our words are just superficial.

The daughters of Jerusalem begin to question the maid about her Beloved, not for a description of Him, but how He is different from any other beloved.

So begins the most marvellous description of the Lord.

Some tell us that there is a picture of God on every page of the Bible, which I believe is true. Daniel, an early prophet had several visions of the Angel Gabriel, but one outstanding vision of the

Lord God as he was standing on the banks of the River Tigris
described in Daniel 10 v 5.

I looked up and there was a man dressed in white linen,
with a belt of the finest gold tied round his waist. His body
was like chrysalite, his face like lightening, his eyes like
flaming torches, his arms and legs like burnished bronze
and his voice like the sound of a multitude. I had no
strength left, my face turned deathly pale and I was
helpless.

St. John who was banished into exile at the age of 90, had a
similar vision which he described in the book of Revelation:

I saw someone like the son of man dressed in a robe
reaching down to his feet with a golden sash round his
chest. His head and hair were like white wool as white as
snow, and his eyes were like blazing fire. His feet were like
blazing bronze glowing in a furnace, and his voice was like
rushing water. In his right hand he held seven stars, and
out of his mouth was a double-edged sword. His face was
like the sun shining in all its brilliance.
When I saw him I fell at his feet as though dead. Then he
placed his right hand on me and said, 'I am the Living One;
I was dead and behold I am alive for ever and ever!
And I hold the keys of death and Hades.

Love Divine

On his journey to Damascus, Paul was suddenly thrown to the ground in the Shekinah Glory of the Lord, who spoke personally to him and thish was the beginning of his life as one of the greatest followers and preachers in the early church. Again Paul speaks of a tremendous light, such as he had never experienced before. This was the beginning of a complete turnaround in his life, after being the greatest persecutor he became the greatest saint.

The writer now begins the most wonderful description of God the Father in Jesus Christ His Son.

V.10: My love is radiant and ruddy, outstanding amongst
ten thousand.
His head is pure gold, his hair as black as a raven.
His eyes are like doves, by the water streams washed in
milk, mounted as jewels.
His cheeks are like beds of spice yielding perfume
His lips are like lilies dripping with myrrh.
His arms are rods of gold set with chrysolite,
His body is like polished ivory decorated with sapphires,
His legs are pillars of marble set on bases of gold,
His appearance is like Lebanon, choice as its cedars.
His mouth is sweetness itself, He is altogether lovely.
This is my Beloved, this is my friend, O daughters of
Jerusalem.

Remember, they did not ask her how he 'looked', but how he 'differed' from any other beloved. It is as we look behind the beauty of his features that we begin to see the likeness of God.

162

Chapter 5

When the Lord told Samuel to go to Jesse of Bethlehem and to offer a sacrifice, He was also told to tell Jesse that He would anoint one of his sons to be king. So Jesse brought his sons before Samuel to be chosen and anointed. The Lord told Jesse 'Do not look at the things man looks at. Man looks at the outward appearance, but the Lord looks at the heart.' After all the sons of Jesse had stood before Samuel, Jesse was asked to fetch his youngest son who was a shepherd looking after the sheep. When this son stood before Samuel, he knew that he was the man fit to become King David. Samuel as a prophet of God could see the inward heart and nature of this youngest son. He was described as, 'Ruddy with a fine appearance and handsome features.'. This is the same word that is used in the Song of Solomon, 'ruddy,' and from it we can assume that the face of her Beloved had the healthy look of one who spends his time in the open country, that He is young with a lively countenance and with normal attractive features.

My Beloved is radiant and ruddy, outstanding among ten thousand

These two colours, radiant and ruddy distinguish Him and mark Him out. The meaning of the word 'radiant' is dazzling bright, it is 'dazzling white, bright as illuminated by the sun.' When Jesus took Peter, James and John up a high mountain and He was transfigured before them, they also saw Elijah and Moses and all their faces shone like the sun, and their clothes became 'glistening, intensely white as no fuller on earth could bleach, as a dazzling white light'. Then the disciples became covered with a bright cloud and God confirmed to them 'This is my Son, with whom I am well pleased. Listen to Him!'

The meaning of the word 'ruddy 'also refers to the colour red; to show blood or to dye or make red.' The one name which above all other names Jesus Christ is known is 'The Lamb'- the sacrifice of God. John the Baptist calls Him 'The Lamb of God who takes away the sins of the world.' It is to the pure spotless Lamb of God. The colour white is the symbol of Christ's pure humanity. Not only is He white but He is red. The colour of the spilt blood on the cross from the spotless Lamb of God who was and still is 'the perfect sufficient sacrifice of God.' We must not be so taken up with the dazzling white, that we forget that without the red (which is the colour of His death), His coming to earth would have availed nothing.

Outstanding among ten thousand.

The number 'ten' signifies an indefinitely large number, and 'thousand' signifies an infinite vast and innumerable number. If the infinitely vast number, symbolized by 'thousand', should be multiplied indefinitely, symbolized by 'Ten', then the result represented is of an innumerable host of all the angels and archangels of Heaven, together with all the renowned who have ever been on earth. If we remember that the vital union which God has put between Christ, who is the 'Chief of ten thousand' and us, and we are members of His Body on earth we have this great power and goodness working through us as we are available for Him. He is the one we love.

His head is purest gold, His hair is wavy and black as a raven.

Gold in the Bible always speaks of the majesty, the purity and the omniscience of our Holy God.

Paul trying to describe Him to the church in Colossi says :

He is the image of the invisible God, the first-born of all creation; for in Him all things were created, in heaven and on earth, visible and invisible, whether thrones or dominions or principalities or authorities – all things were created through him and for Him. He is before all things, and in Him all things hold together. He is the head of the body, the church; He is the beginning, the first born from the dead, that in everything He might be pre-eminent For in Him all the fullness of God was pleased to dwell.[27]

These verses written by Paul to the church in Colossi say everything.

His hair is uncovered and is the head of authority, and as His hair is described as black and wavy, it is the thick hair of manhood without any grey, and speaks of the eternal youth of the Beloved, the Jesus who will never grow old, and who will be with us throughout eternity.

In Psalm 110 v3,4 He is described as 'the God who inhabits Eternity, He wears white hair which is the mark of the Ancient of

---

[27] Colossians 1: 16-18.

Love Divine

Days,' and this is how both Daniel and John in Patmos saw Him. But the maid describes her Beloved with black wavy hair. Jesus Christ is the immortal one.

V.12: His eyes are like doves by the winter streams,
Washed in milk, mounted like jewels.

The eye is the symbol of knowledge and understanding, and here described is the eye of one who sees all things. Both Daniel and John described the eyes of the Ancient of Days as flames of fire, but here the tender compassion of God is seen in the eyes of the Beloved. They are as gentle as a dove when He looks upon those He has redeemed. They are bathed in the milk of God's Word, in tenderness and compassion as they look towards us. His compassion is infinite, His tenderness is unfathomable and His long suffering for us is everlasting. In some translations His eyes are 'fitly set'. They are not hooded eyes, or have any hint of a squint or injustice. As the God of truth they may be piercing and discerning to those who nurture unworthy thoughts, envious thoughts, and thoughts that are injurious to others. It is quite wonderful to sit and picture His face and look deeply into the eyes of Jesus. I wonder if we all see the same face? His eyes will be dark as an Eastern Jew. Walter Wangerin in his book *GOD* always describes them as 'dark eyes flecked with gold'- eyes that are sparkling with life; exactly as I imagine them to be!

V.13: His cheeks are like beds of spice, yielding perfume
His lips are like lilies dripping with myrrh.

The cheeks represent the whole of the face in this verse. I have mentioned the connection between the herbs and spices with the Beloved and His bride. The incense for the temple worship was made up of equal parts of sweet herbs and fragrant spices. Every pang of suffering that the Lord suffered carrying out the will of His Father was sweet incense before the face of God. When the Jews buffeted Him, mocking Him and deriding Him, to His Father the cheeks were a bed of spices and sweet herbs. As Jesus went through every phase of His passion, the mocking by the Roman Soldiers, the insult when they braided a crown of thorns on His head and clothed Him with a purple robe and spat upon Him, His Father must have looked upon Him and received the fragrance of His Son's precious herbs and spices. When those who know and love the Lord with their whole hearts, and recall in their minds a minutiae of the pain and horror of the cross, and the smiting of the Lord as He carried His cross, we remember the sweet herbs and spices offered up to His Father. No matter how sorrowful we may feel, we know that He went to Calvary according to His Fathers will, so that we, the fallen world could come before a Holy God.

His lips are like lilies dripping with myrrh.

The lilies with their beautiful whiteness and red throats symbolize health and beauty.

Love Divine

All the words coming from the lips of Jesus were full of health and wisdom to those who heard them. Only from Him were words that could heal sick souls. Above all others, it was said of Jesus that He was God's ambassador to fallen and sin cursed humanity. When our Lord first came on earth as a young man those about Him marvelled at the words of grace that He spoke, 'for He spoke as one who had authority and not as other men.' Luke tells us that the scribes and Pharisees began to provoke Him and press upon Him vehemently to make Him speak so that they could accuse Him, but He spoke with such wisdom, that 'they were not able to take hold of anything before the people.'

1 Peter 2 v 22, 23:

He committed no sin, and no deceit was found in His mouth. When they hurled insults at Him, He did not retaliate; when He suffered, He made no threats. Instead He entrusted himself to one who judges justly.

Lips ... dripping with myrrh.

'His lips dripping with myrrh' causes us again to remember the pain of the cross and the price that Jesus paid for us. We can say these words so quickly and easily, perhaps without much thought, but without those lips saying 'You are forgiven; I have paid the price for you so that you can come into the presence of my

Father, a Holy God, all your sins are forgiven,' how could we live today?

Only when the Father gave our Lord the words to speak during His passion did He reply to His accusers. His silence as He carried out the will of God must have been as liquid myrrh to the Father.

V.14: His arms are rods of gold, set with chrysolite.

The arms of gold again point to the divinity of God. Everything that Jesus did was according to the will of God. His arms of gold holding us in safety and love give as a quiet peace, and as we settle in His embrace He will guide us and show us the way. Chrysolite is a yellowish-green precious stone that has a golden shine. They are not just gold but arms prepared by His loving Father for the embrace He will have for all of us. Sometimes they may hold us tight in admonishment directing us to the right path, but we will always find that His ways bring fruit to us and deepen our relationship with Him. This verse also describes them as 'rods', which speak of firmness and strength.

His body is like polished ivory decorated with sapphires.

This is Jesus the Son of man and the Son of God. Ivory is pure and beautiful. Ivory that is cut and shaped is another symbol of Christ's body. It is beautiful because God prepared it for His only beloved Son to dwell in. Though in the eyes of man, 'He has no form or comeliness and no beauty that none should desire Him.' In this description His body is bright because he is the Son of God.

Love Divine

He appeared to the Jews as a poor and weak of body, of an unknown man who was despised and rejected, but to the Father and the bride it was beautiful ivory inset with sapphires. The blue sapphires are a symbol of His heavenly nature. Although He dwelt in a despised human body, in Him dwelt all the fullness of the Godhead. In the 45th Psalm, the pure human body given up to God is described as an ivory palace. Ivory has to be carved and shaped, which symbolizes all the different ways that He gave His life for us. He had no home or fixed bed to sleep on and was often tired and hungry, but His greatest desire was always that we should come to know the Father.

Not only is the body of the Lord described as wrought ivory during His time on earth but His mystical body, the church is still on earth and is being wrought and perfected as shining ivory. While we are here on earth we will receive all the preparation and working of the Holy Spirit before we receive our new body in heaven. Again the blue sapphires point us towards our Heavenly destination. Because we are in Jesus, we are upheld by His love, which passes all understanding. How important it is that our attitude should never be 'stiff-necked 'towards the Holy Spirit and the words of our God.

V.15: His legs are pillars of marble set on bases of gold.

The legs of our Lord were as pillars, strong, symmetrical, and beautiful; they would never falter or fail. In all the works that God does it is 'exceeding abundantly' above all that man can think. Not only was God's plan to bring man back to the Garden of Eden, but

170

He made a plan for us to be brought to the heavenly garden. He has lifted man from sin and degradation and made him a new creation in Christ Jesus. He has set us over the earth, and all the beasts and creatures upon the earth. He has raised mankind above all principalities and powers. He has made him heir of God and joint heir with Jesus Christ.

He has made man a temple of God, and has come to each of His children in His triune personality to take His abode in each one of them. As we meditate on the grace of God and His mercy towards us we can only re-commit our lives to Him.

The pillars of marble are a symbol of Christ's omnipotence, and upon them the salvation of the world rests. Because the leg is an emblem of strength, God did not allow the soldiers to break the legs of the Lord, 'not a bone was broken'. Neither can any burden nor weight be beyond His power, which is infinite just as He is infinite.

The feet or bases of the pillar are set on bases of pure gold.

The sandals He wore were symbolic of pure gold, again a picture of the divine. As a pillar is set in a socket to make it steadfast so the legs of the Lord are steadfast in the power, and divinity of God. Silver, biblically, is a symbol of atonement, as it has to be beaten into shape, but Jesus Christ, the Son of God needs no atonement to uphold Him and make Him steadfast. His strength and all that He accomplishes are upheld by the pure Godhead the fullness of which dwells in Him alone.

Love Divine

His appearance is like Lebanon, choice as its cedars.

The bride has described the One, whom her soul loves, describing Him from head to foot, remembering the pathway along which He has led her and the power of the cross which she is beginning to understand, and also that as part of the Kingdom of God, there will be a role for her to fulfil. The tall mountain of Lebanon was always crowned with snow, and the white sandstone could be seen from a distance, and as she sees this grandeur and majesty she is reminded of the Son of Man and Son of God. Even though Jesus was despised and rejected by man while He was here on earth, Satan and his demons recognised His Majesty as they saw Him cast out evil spirits and heal; they trembled as the Lord cast out evil spirits and raised some from the dead.

So often it seems that we come to our Lord as though He was a man like ourselves. We realise and possibly meditate upon the cross, and thank the Lord for His sacrifice and our salvation. We recognise the goodness and perfection in Him, but we lack the reverence and fear that He is God. We must not forget that He who dwelt upon the earth in the body that God prepared for Him also inhabits Eternity; He is in heaven and we are on earth with His Holy Spirit within us.

We must not only remember His fragrance here on earth, but worship Him not only as the Son of man but as the Son of God. We must behold His majesty and worship Him. Maybe we need to ask God that we may not only see His hair, curly and black as a raven, the symbol of His manhood, but that we may also see Him as the 'Ancient of Days.' The more closely we draw to Him, the

172

more intimately we know Him, the more clearly we see Him in His majesty; and we find that we begin to see Him as the 'Ancient of Days', and are brought into a closer intimacy with Him as a 'Man of Sorrows.

V.16: His mouth is sweetness itself, he is altogether lovely.

In the first chapter of the Song of Solomon, the bride prays for a close intimate relationship with her Beloved: 'Let Him kiss me with the kisses of the mouth.' It is a revelation of His love that passes all knowledge; of such joy that is as full of glory; of such peace that passes all understanding; of such faith and love that will bind us to Him in an increasing oneness that the maid still yearns to experience in a deeper way.

He is altogether lovely.

There is nothing about Him that any one of us would change or have otherwise. He is precious, our all in all. To the bride of Christ there is no loveliness nor beauty in any other, there is no spot or blemish in Him, in all things He is delightful...it is when we set our lives to know Him; as we go through any persecution for His sake, that we receive all He has for us, and He becomes altogether lovely. As we pray for all those around the world who are suffering great pain and deprivation because of their love for Him, we can only pray that they will have a deeper revelation of Jesus in whatever difficult cruel situation they are experiencing.

Love Divine

And pray too that they will experience even more of the loveliness of the Godhead than perhaps we will ever know.

This is my Beloved, this is my friend, O daughters of Jerusalem.

The maid desires that everyone should know that this one, whom she has been describing, this is the one who loves her; and this is the one whom she loves. He is the one who proved His love for her by dying so that she might be His bride. He is drawing her closer to Himself so that she may discern His beauties and experience his preciousness, which He is waiting to reveal to every soul who will come to Him.

When Christ hides His face for a season, whether it is to quicken our faith, or because of some infidelity on our part, it always seems that His beauty breaks in on our souls as never before. Maybe we have been enjoying His presence because we do believe, but we have become indolent and careless of our relationship. We may take our communion with Him as a matter of course, or indeed with irreverence. Sometimes it may seem that it is impossible to lose the closeness and our touch with the Lord because of our past life, we do still love Him, but we have become careless with our relationship, and other facts are taking over our life.

When again we hear Him at the door, and turn to Him and to our dismay find that He has gone, we need to repent and go after him through prayer and reading the Word of God. It is then as we listen to the shepherds, and seek Him through prayer in humility we find Him again and begin to see Him more clearly than we have ever seen Him before. When we remember that He was man and has been tempted in all points such as we experience and knows all our infirmities, He in His perfect love will reveal Himself to us again

To those who turn back to Him and find that He is altogether lovely and there is no defect in him. We rejoice that there is no change in him, for He is the unchangeable One. However unsteady man is, however we are, our Beloved is always the same, and there is no variableness in Him, or shadow cast by His turning.

He is our Beloved and also our Friend, our Friend who will never let us down. Human friends may be untrue, and may fail and disappoint us. This Friend, this One whose beauty and attributes we have been considering will never fail us.

A most precious hymn written by Isaac Watts (1674-1748) to illustrate Paul's letter to the Galatians Ch.6 v14 sums up our response to the bride's description of her Beloved:

Were the whole realm of nature mine,
That were an offering far too small;
Love so amazing, so divine,
Demands my soul, my life, my all.

Love Divine

CHAPTER SIX

Verse 1 begins with the reaction of the friends of the maid to her description of her Beloved.

Where has your beloved gone, most beautiful of women?
Which way did your Beloved turn, that we may look for
Him with you?

The first time the bride spoke to the daughters of Jerusalem she told them of her blackness and unworthiness and asked them not to judge her or the Lord by the defects they saw in her. She always addresses these daughters of Jerusalem as those who are watching her, and are not enemies, nor are they true followers of the Lord. We now begin to see the result of a consistent consecrated life seen by those who have been watching the bride since she came to the Lord.

Many years ago our family opened a shop and restaurant in York, and when it came to buying the tables and chairs for the restaurant I could not think why I felt so unhappy at the thought of just buying new tables and chairs of a uniform size, so we decided to buy second hand furniture, which meant that we had various sized tables which included our own long refectory table. The wonderful result, which we could never have envisaged, was that when there was a queue waiting for a place for lunch, people often graciously offered to share their table, and many interesting conversations came about as Christians 'chattered the Lord.' Many times after someone had come for lunch or a coffee they asked us if they could buy a book to find out more about our faith. Perhaps they had overheard something, or had been invited to join a conversation. Fortunately we had several small tables for those who wanted to be on their own. One day two ladies from *The Tatler* came in for lunch. We were not aware of this until a friend very kindly sent me a copy of the magazine, with their printed article on one of the pages. Everything that they said about the food and atmosphere of the *Mustard Seed* was very encouraging, but they did remark that 'Some of the tables were a little wobbly'!

The friends of the maid have watched her as she was smitten and humiliated by those who should have comforted and supported her, and they have wondered why she has not stopped her search, but had quickened her steps to find Him. With amazement they see that the opposition makes her love the Lord more devotedly and seek Him more zealously. The more she was opposed, the more eagerly she enquired of all she met and asked them to tell Him that she was 'sick with love' because of her separation from Him. She not only regrets the indolence that caused this separation, but she was deeply repentant in her heart; so that nothing could satisfy her but the Lord.

She was echoing in her heart the words of Paul when he was writing to the Christian Church in Philippi. In his letter he explained his ambitions and his life:

I count all things but loss for the excellency of the
knowledge of Christ Jesus my Lord, for whom I suffered the
loss of all things, and count them but refuse; that I may

gain Christ, and be found in Him, not having any
righteousness of my own that comes from the law, but that
which comes through faith in Christ. The righteousness that
comes from God and is by faith.
I want to know Christ and the power of His resurrection
and the fellowship of sharing in His sufferings, becoming
like Him in His death, and so somehow to attain to the
resurrection from the dead.[28]
V.2: My beloved is gone to His garden to the beds of spices,
to browse in the garden and to gather lilies.

Historically, this is speaking of the body of Jesus Christ lying in the sepulchre on the bed of herbs and spices. We cannot comprehend the pain, the suffering and unbelief that the disciples must have felt as they watched Him hanging on the cross; for three hours they stood and watched Him dying there; and then realising, as the soldiers took Him down, that He really was dead. They had seen Him perform many miracles, they saw Him rebuke death, and command it to bring back the life of someone it had taken. They had listened to His teachings and had been with Him for three years, even if they did not really comprehend all that He was saying. The reproach and shame as they saw Him hang there so filled their thoughts, and the grief was so great that their eyes were blinded to the joy that was to come. If He had come down from the cross we would never have had our supreme salvation, which

---

[28] Philippians 3 vv 7-11.

Love Divine

could only come through His death and resurrection. There would have been no redemption for even one soul.

V.3: I am my Beloved's, and my Beloved is mine; He browses among the lilies.

As the bride describes the beauties of her Beloved, and she remembers that He has gone to his garden she feels encouraged in her heart as she remembers the precious experiences they have had together. She is feeling more self-assured as though she has said, 'I am *for* my Beloved and He is *for* me'.

If our desire is to be a worthy child of God, and above everything want to walk in His ways and live our lives according to His will then no matter what we may be confronted with in life we will have the inner assurance that God is our rock, that He knows what is happening to us and that with Him we will come through the difficulty.

V.4: You are beautiful my love, as Tirzah, lovely as Jerusalem, majestic as troops with banners.

The Beloved is again addressing the bride, and His love is shown through every description He gives of her beauty. The meaning of 'Tirzah' is 'pleasant or well-pleasing'. It is a city in a beautiful situation and was chosen as the royal city of the kings of Canaan. The city was built upon a hill and was bright and shining from the sun on the beautiful white marble of the walls. We are reminded of the Lord's description of His true followers in Matthew 5 v 14:

You are the light of the world. A city set upon a hill cannot be hidden. Even so let your light shine before; that they see your good works, and glorify your Father in Heaven.

Originally this beautiful city was filled with idolatry, wickedness and abomination by the kings and their courts, until it was eventually captured by the Hebrews and turned into the royal city of the kings of Israel. We can see that this is like our own lives until we are taken over by the Lord and 'captured' into His life. The comparison is to the earthly Jerusalem with its compacted streets, harmony within the high street walls and beautiful palaces and glorious temple. It is a symbol of the many tribes and people, the fellowship, the perfect unity of the living stones of the New Jerusalem.

Terrible as an army of banners.

This verse refers to a huge army holding up the banners of the soldiers in a newly fortified city. It is the wonderful grace of God that we can look upon all opposition, all conflict, all persecution, all attacks of the enemy however they may come, as opportunities to add to the precious banners that we can uphold for God. She is not represented here as downtrodden by the enemy, or defeated, but as one who can walk upright before the Lord. Hudson Taylor, the great missionary who started the China Inland Mission in the

Love Divine

19 Century, eventually had thousands of workers in that vast country, all supported by prayer, and gifts of money from the U.K. Daily he had many problems and was often without money and had no food, but his God was only a prayer away. He said, 'All our difficulties are a platform from which God works.'

V.5: Turn your eyes away from me, they overwhelm me.
Your hair is like a flock of goats descending from Gilead

After her long search the maid has eventually found her Beloved and conquered Him with one glance of her eyes, which are searching earnestly for Him. There are many examples in the Old Testament where we can read of such fervour and singe mindedness. Jacob, when he wrestled with the angel of God until daybreak, and would not let Him go until God blessed him. The angel who was God Himself could have just turned away but Jacob would not let him go, until He touched Jacob's hip so that he would forever have to walk with a limp and have to lean upon God. After Jacob's determination and fervent wrestling with God he received the blessing he sought from his heavenly Father. Thereafter he was called Israel, and became a devout servant who changed from a man who was always trying to force his will on every situation, to a man who leaned only on God.

Moses had to intercede many times for God's people until Jehovah said, 'Now leave me alone so that my anger may burn against them and that I may destroy them. Then I will make you into a great nation.'[29] While Moses was up in the mountain talking to God, the Israelites, the chosen people had built a golden calf and had begun to fall down and worship it. Moses pleaded with God to let the people reach the Promised Land. We read too of how beautifully God yields to Abraham as he interceded for those who were not wicked in Sodom and Gomorrah. Do we sometimes doubt that God hears us, or are we too weak to prevail in prayer?

Vv.6-7: Your hair is like a flock of goats descending from Gilead

Your teeth are like a flock of sheep coming up from the washing.

Each has its twin, not one is alone.

Your temples behind your veil are like the halves of a pomegranate.

Once before in chapter 4 the Beloved has compared the bride's hair to a flock of goats. But we now see that as time has passed everything is not quite the same. In the sixth chapter He again describes her hair, her teeth, and blushing temples. These are the points of the beauty of the bride that have been marred and partially dimmed since He last described her. She has lain down and slept without thought of Him, and she has enjoyed the admiration of those about her. She has shrunk from arising to admit her Beloved when he was outside her door, when He called her to open the door of her life so that he may speak to her.

---

[29] Exodus 32 v 10

Love Divine

In this chapter He does not speak of her lips that are like a thread of scarlet, and her mouth or speech that is so beautiful. He does not speak of the strength of her tower-like neck, and the strong trophies of war and victory; her breasts which represent the equal quality of faith and love, which we should attain in our lives. Although she has been indolent, He still calls her His dove, His undefiled. Her mouth and speech are not *so* sweet and uplifting as before, but her love and faith in her Lord has not departed. It is her own indolence and disobedience that has weakened and marred her separation from the Lord. It is not the world that has caused this to happen but those who were called by His name, those who smote her when she was distraught in the city streets looking for Him. She has not been feeding upon the living word of God as she faithfully did before, nor has she been speaking to Him in prayer. Through the admiration of others she has lost some of her humility, she has become self-satisfied, not with her beauty, but with her knowledge of the Lord. She knows His voice, but is self-satisfied with her relationship, so that she has not entered into a deeper relationship with Him than those around her. The Lord does not speak to her of those symbols of her beauty that arise through cleansing and purity and her desire to be separated from the world bearing His name; but He speaks of those things that have been marred through her slumber and concentrating upon her own desires.

He begins to teach her by withdrawing from her the very experiences through which she has become self-confident. As He withdraws His presence and remains silent to her cries and prayers, she quickly arises; there is nothing that can stop her until she has overtaken Him, and again hears His voice and looks upon His beauty. As the watchmen smote her and cast out her name as evil, because of their jealousy towards her, and tore her cloak, she realises all that she has lost. She begins to search the Scriptures and claim the promises of God, and she receives again a clearer revelation and knowledge of God and of the living Word. After repenting and seeking Him in contrition, and refusing to be turned aside by the opposition and blows of the watchman, she again turns to his Word, and receives a clearer revelation and knowledge of the one she has lost. Her teeth of faith begin to grow strong and even. The humiliation and indignity which she suffered as she ran after Him bring to her brow the blush and colour of the pomegranate; and this humility and modesty are hidden under the veil of her hair. Her Beloved again speaks to her and now His words of commendation are far beyond anything he has said so far. Never before has He likened her to the beautiful city of Tirzah, and the beautiful compact city of Jerusalem. Before she had been placed where all eyes could see her, but she was not yet steadfast. While her light had been bright, it had not yet become steady and able to pierce through the shadows and valleys. Her life did not show conviction to those who were not believers and not following her Beloved. Since she arose and opened the door, since she went out into the darkness to look for Him she has attained a greater stability and steadfastness of light. She has entered into a greater unity and fellowship with her Beloved. Her hair has again become long and beautiful like a flock of goats lying on the sides of Mount

Love Divine

Gilead, her teeth have been strengthened, and become like a flock of ewes that have come up from the washing; her humility, hidden away by her locks of separation and consecration, has been perfected. He has likened her to the light that stood white and bright upon a hill, and to the compact beautiful city of Jerusalem filled with many people of different races and beliefs where His temple is built.

Vv 8-9: Sixty queens there may be and eighty concubines,
and virgins without number,
But my dove my perfect one is unique
the only daughter of her mother, the favourite of the one
who bore her.
The maidens saw her and called her blessed;
the queens and concubines praised her.

The same thought that was brought out in the second chapter is expressed in these verses.

Though there are three score (an indefinite number) of queens, and four score, (again an indefinite number) of concubines, together with a vast number of virgins, the Beloved declares that His dove is but one. In the second chapter we are told that all the daughters are as thorns when compared to His bride, who is the only lily. All the queens and concubines of earthly courts, all the virgins on earth are only a multitude, and of no importance as compared to the countless multitude in His glistening robes of righteousness that make up the bride of Christ. As the will and purposes of God are worked out in each one of us, all shall come

186

together and make up the undefiled and spotless bride of the Lamb of God. This unity does not come from trying to be one with one another, but by being one with the Lord, and as we enter our union with Him, we are united with each other in the perfect unity, which is born in Him, and given by Him. The special part of this, is that it is not imagination, but is eternal reality. Not only are we the body of Christ made *one in* Christ, but we are *one with* Christ, for He is the Head, and we are members of His body, of His flesh, and of His bones. So often in our lives we can be caused to gasp when the Lord does something so personal it is just as if we are the only person in the world.

V.10: Who is this that appears like the dawn,
fair as the moon, bright as the sun,
majestic as the stars in procession?

These are the words of the daughters of Jerusalem, who are questioning with amazement the change that they are seeing in the bride; they are seeing something upon her and within her that they have never seen before. They cannot understand the illumination, which is beginning to shine from within her, which they have likened to the first rays of dawn that tinge and lighten the sky, and some begin to discern that this light, which is beginning to appear with such beauty upon her is not from herself, but is a supernatural light hidden away within her.

Several years ago a group of us were involved in a work in the church where we opened a restaurant and book/gift shop as a place where people could come to eat and talk or buy cards toys etc. All those who worked there were willing at that time to put their careers on hold, to trust God for their needs, only taking for themselves a few pounds a week. Our aim was to seek first His Kingdom, and His righteousness. Our aim was that during our contact in serving and helping others through prayer and the work of the Holy Spirit, conversations would open up, and we would have the chance to speak of the reality of the Lord in our lives. We had cards on the tables explaining about the work we were doing, and because the city was always full of tourists even in the winter months, we had many foreign visitors who came especially to find us.

Several times I was asked about the light that others saw on the faces of those who worked in this very busy shop. Obviously we were not aware of this, and I most certainly would not compare ourselves to the nurses who worked in the hospitals of Mother Theresa, but those working in the shop had too laid aside their desires and way of life to accomplish a work for the Lord.

The daughters of Jerusalem are at different stages of perfection and preparation with their walk with the Lord. Those who are most mature and who have been following closely the pathway of the maid will discern more easily the light that they see within her. The bride not only looks as fair as the dawn but also is as bright and as clear as the sun. Proverbs 4 v 18 says, 'The path of the righteous is like the first gleam of dawn, shining ever brighter till the full light of day.'

This light maybe difficult to understand, but it can be seen. I saw this in the faces and the demeanour of the nurses working for

Mother Theresa in Bombay (or Mumbai as the town is now called). These young women who had given up all earthly possessions for the love of the Lord, were quietly going about their work from bed to bed in a peace that was past all understanding. The wards were huge, with the beds very close together but there was no sense of rush or haste. We were asked to join them in prayer in a simple room just as we might invite people into our own home, except there was practically no furniture. Also, just as when we sometimes meet a Christian and immediately feel that we know them, it was the same with the nuns; we prayed to the same God, just another part of the Body of Christ kneeling together.

Vv.11, 12: I went down to the grove of nut trees,
to look at the new growth in the valley,
To see if the vines had budded or the pomegranates were in bloom.
Before I realised it, my desire set me among the royal chariots of my people.

A friend who had a plantation of nut trees near Jerusalem, and was disappointed that they did not bare much fruit, suddenly remembered this verse, and removed them to a grove further down the hill where they began to flourish. No word or description is wasted in the Bible, sometimes a translation might be a little dubious, but if you can go back to the original scripts nothing is amiss.

This is the third garden that is mentioned in this book. The first is found in Ch.2 v 12, which is the garden of flowers and immature fruit, a time of late spring and early summer. In this garden, everything brings a promise of a full harvest but at this time nothing is perfected. The second garden is an autumnal garden, and it begins in Ch.5 v 1. In this garden, all is perfect and ripe, with many spices, which are all associated with the Lord.

The third garden is at the end of winter, just before spring. There are nuts from the year before; the green plants are about to flower, and the buds on the vines and flowers, and also the pomegranates are about to appear. As I have said earlier, the 'garden' refers to the Kingdom of Heaven; and the four different descriptions portray the Kingdom of Heaven in different processes of growth and perfection.

Historically this is speaking of the Dispensation of Grace, and the fulfilment of the Word of God concerning the coming of Jesus Christ, His redemptive work on the cross, and the outpouring of His Holy Spirit which began on the day of Pentecost and has continued ever since. The nuts speak of the promises of God, and it was into a veritable garden of nuts that Jesus led His disciples into after His resurrection. He explained to the disciples all that they would accomplish in His Kingdom, He told them of all the spiritual gifts that would enable them to heal and bring many others to know Him.

Before He ascended to the Father; Beginning from Moses and from all the prophets, He interpreted to them in all the Scriptures and the prophecies concerning Himself, and He opened their minds that they might understand all the Scriptures.

Luke 24 vv 27 and 45: 'And beginning with Moses and all the prophets, He explained to them what was said in all the Scriptures concerning himself... Then He opened their minds so that they could understand the Scriptures.'

Nuts cannot be eaten until the shells are cracked open, and then we can taste the sweetness of the fruit. Unless the Lord opens up our understanding of the Word of God, it is impossible to fully understand the Scriptures. When the Holy Spirit, the Teacher and the one who leads us into all truth reveals to us the real meanings that lie at the root of every Scripture, He will bring us to a deep understanding and new revelations of God's word. Also as we sit at the feet of scholars, and read the words of Biblical saints we can be inspired, and encouraged to seek further the Gospel of Christ.[30]

A great teacher and man of God whose ministry was worldwide would sometimes greet us in the morning excited with a new revelation he had just come to realise in the Bible and I remembered thinking, 'If he, after all the years of his ministry and all the books he has written can still be excited by the Word of God I have only just scratched the surface.' The Bible is the one book that libraries have been filled explaining it, and yet a small child can read it and be absorbed by the words that are written. With reverence and gratitude we must praise God that His Spirit searches all things, literally the depths of God, and reveals them to us. To those who earnestly desire and yield to God and pray for His instruction and counsel that they might interpret the Word,

---

[30] 1 Cor.2 v 14.

Love Divine

they become aware of the charm and wonder and enter into its mysteries.

V.12: Before I realised it, my desire set me among the royal chariots of my people.

Or, 'made me like the chariots of Ammi-nadib' in some translations. As the maid is busy with all that the Lord has set before her she is caught up in His presence. Ammi-nadib are two words that open up the meaning. Ammi is referring to 'troops or a company of people congregated together or made one'; and the literal meaning of the last word is 'The prince.' So the interpretation that we can take is: 'The people or company that have become one, and are the chariots of the Lord'

As we read in Psalm 68 v17-18:

The chariots of God are tens of thousands, and thousands of thousands:
The Lord has come from Sinai into His sanctuary
When you ascended on high, you led captives in your train;
you received gifts from men,
Even from the rebellious – that you O Lord God, might dwell there.

This experience of the bride is not an uplift that only lasts for a short time, one of those times of blessing when we enter into the presence of the Lord but do not abide there. It is referring to a time when we are aware of the Lord with us, and are aware of His help in a specific work or ministry, but are also aware of a more lasting and deeper communion with Him, and with the company that has been made one in Him; that company that is called the 'chariots of the Prince' because of their courage and abandonment to the Prince of Peace. At these times if we know that many saints in the Kingdom are behind us in prayer perhaps from believers from all over the world working together with the Lord, we can feel that there is a great power behind us. If we are praying for a particular catastrophe, or for those in imprisonment for their faith, or people who are abandoned and left homeless and hungry because of greed and misrule from those in power, we pray and may feel like a small voice in the wilderness, yet it is always so encouraging to know our prayers are echoing the prayers of many others.

So often when we are engrossed in the work of the Lord and all that we feel we should accomplish, we let the 'work' of the Lord steal away the anointing and (to use an old fashioned word) the unction upon our own souls. The energy and activity of 'building up 'others, hospitality and caring for those around us, or maybe teaching and preaching, causes 'the work' to sooth us into a vain belief that the activity is really of the foremost importance in our life, when our top priority should be our relationship with the Lord and prayer.

When I was younger with a home and family and with what often seemed like so many other commitments during the day, I used to think life would be so much easier if I did not have so many things to think about. Then I could have 'quiet times' and more time for prayer. Alas I am now alone but I still have to put aside a committed time for prayer and Bible reading, otherwise I still tend to think I have not the time, or just fall asleep! I once asked a very busy committed leader of the church how she managed with a young family, plus her extended family, and she said, 'As I wash up, or am tackling a boring job I always put my thoughts to a particular verse or thought in the Bible, and I listen to the Lord.'

V.12: The friends of the maid call her 'Come back, come back, O Shulammite.
Come back that we may gaze on you!

The daughters of Jerusalem watch the bride, and they realise that her spirit is completely taken up with her new life. They do not understand what has happened, but they know that a separation has taken place between her and them, which is more that a bodily separation. Although she is living and moving among them, and they see her at her earthly tasks and God given work, they realise that the maid has moved beyond them and their understanding, and they see that she has deeper priorities. She has a peaceful presence about her. This peace does not come to her if she is neglecting the Word of God, and if she is not caring for the welfare of those about her. Nor is it experienced when she is absorbed in 'Christian work' and all her everyday tasks. It is through chastening and suffering she has been brought to the place where she is given over more and more to the Lord, and her desire is only to seek and accomplish His will. No matter what she is doing, her communion with Him and her devotion to Him are increasing all the time. If we serve Him with intermittent zeal our soul does not grow and thrive, and when we are indifferent to Him we are not watered by His love. It is when we have been subdued, refined and chastened, when love of self and the world has gone, that we learn to abide in touch with Him at all times, and in all places or surroundings. This does not mean she must cut herself off from those around her; she must be with those who do not believe, friends and relations as part of the community, but with an inward peace and a love for those about her.

It is not until others see the presence of the Lord within her that those about her call her by the name 'Shulammite' which was name of the bride of Solomon. 'Shulammite' is the feminine of 'Solomon' and means the daughter of peace. She receives this new name, which is how the daughters of Jerusalem address her, even though she is unconscious that this is the first time that they have called her Shulammite. She accepts the name that speaks of her oneness with the Lord.

Why would you gaze upon the Shulammite, as the dance of Mahanaim?

Or 'as it were on two armies,' the meaning of 'the dance of Mahanaim' There are two expositions of this verse which are generally accepted by students of the Bible. One is that 'the company of two armies' comprises one army that is in heaven and the other those who are still upon the earth. The second interpretation refers to the two hosts, or armies, of light and darkness and the conflict between them. Whichever we accept,

Love Divine

there is a thought of continual warfare. Matthew tells us that Jesus warned us that there would be difficulties, especially with close relationships. 'Do not suppose that I have come to bring peace on earth, I did not come to bring peace but a sword, for I have come to turn a man against his father, a daughter against her mother, a daughter-in-law against her mother in-law -a man's enemies will be the members of his of his own household.'[31] The second exposition refers to the two armies of light and darkness, the warfare between the army of the Lord and the army of Satan, in which the believer is the battlefield. So often it is against those who have stepped out to do their best for their God and Lord that the evil one attacks the hardest. With relentless hatred, Satan tries to bring down those who have made a commitment to the Lord, by devious means so that the faithful might not join the ranks of the overcomers, those who continue to believe and trust. It is when the fierce battle is raging that we need to retreat into Jesus Christ and find that peace within. It is the peace of God, which passes all understanding that garrisons our hearts and keeps guard of the doors of our souls.

It is nearly always in the hard conflict and persecution, that the peace of God flourishes and is perfected. This heavenly peace that comes down from God, is always found within; and God will set it before the doors of our hearts as a sentinel watching a treasure if we are quiet in Him, and take refuge in Him.

---

[31] Matthew 10 v 34-36.

CHAPTER SEVEN

The beauty of the bride as seen by the Daughters of Jerusalem.

V.1: How beautiful are your sandaled feet, O prince's daughter!
Your graceful legs are like jewels, the work of a craftsman's hands.

The daughters begin their description of the bride by describing her feet. Maybe they are remembering the verse, 'Beautiful upon the mountains are the feet of Him who brings good tidings, who speaks of peace, and brings salvation through Jesus Christ.'

In the previous verse we have seen how the maid is taken up with her relationship with the Lord, and it is when we are endeavouring to grow closer to the Lord by the grace of His Holy Spirit, that we can bring hungry souls to the Lord's table and the gospel of peace. The bride's feet are not naked or poorly shod, she has so yielded to the workings of God that her feet are perfectly shod with gospel of peace. The significance of the clothing of the feet for the Christian is the knowledge and appropriation of the gospel into our life; the believers go on from victory to victory. As she goes about the business of her Beloved's vineyards and walks through His gardens, in all her daily walk she is worthy of Him, and every step is beautiful to those who observe her. It is not long ago since the bride had laid aside her shoes; and when her Beloved knocked she was afraid of soiling her feet upon the dusty floor.

Love Divine

Since then she has hastened about the streets searching for Him, she has been smitten by the shepherds who were convicted by her love of the Lord, and now instead of bruised feet she is shod with the gospel of peace, perfectly befitting her as she has come to a greater revelation of the truth.

As we look back to the beginning of our walk with the Lord it is fascinating to see how He so often prepared us for His vineyard when we were not aware of it. I did once ask the Lord what the future held, when I was asked to arrange and cater for a wedding for three hundred. The bride and groom were (and still are) missionaries and we had a team of helpers from the church, and much help from the Lord, to steer us away from disaster. A few years later I found myself planning a shop for a meeting place for visitors from all over the world. When a thought came into my head that maybe we should serve food, I thought, 'No, no, no, I will not tell anybody that!' But then someone said, 'You could serve food, and I will help you.' That particular lady was not available when the time came, but suddenly without any particular advertising, out of the blue came a teacher who was the head of Home Economics in a London school, and she came to us to see if she could help.

Your graceful legs are like jewels, the work of a craftsman's hands.

As in many portions of Scripture, the different parts of the body is really a description of the covering which forms the body, and these descriptions symbolise the beauties and perfections of

198

the Church of Jesus Christ, and which again is set to describe the perfect beauty and full development of a person. Sometimes Scripture uses the adorning of the female form in a descriptive way. The bride of Christ is always pictured as feminine in all her purity and beauty, worthy of the Lord in all His worthiness. However we know that no matter what gender, size, colour or shape we are, we are all equal and part of the body of Christ on earth. Every truth of God, when it is operative in our life is like a jewel; and the Holy Spirit is the skilful Workman who deals, and teaches and leads us into all Truth, until these jewels of God's word and Christ's nature are put on us one by one. As the bride lives out the gospel day by day, she is enabled to walk in victory; and this full goblet that Christ prepared and filled for her, is brought to others through her ministry.

The description of the 'rounded thighs', the 'body' and the 'waist' are beautifully given in Ephesians where the body of Christ is described, to those who are strong in the Lord, and not tossed about like flotsam and rubbish.

There we will no longer be infants, tossed back and forth by the waves, and blown here and there by every wind of teaching, and by the cunning and craftiness in men by their deceitful scheming. Instead, speaking the truth in love, we will in all things grow up into Him who is the Head, that is, Christ. From Him the whole body, joined and held together

Love Divine

by every supporting ligament grows and builds itself in
love, as each part does its work.[32]

The first and primary thought, from which all others evolve, is
the perfect working together and the united strength, which is
operative in the Church through every joint and sinew; every part
doing its work. The thigh is the part of the leg in which lies the
strength for walking or running, or, in other words, it is the seat of
strength for our daily walk. It is as this joint works freely, as the
thigh is perfectly developed and made strong and healthy through
exercise that the whole body is made strong. As the thigh is built
up and strong so it will be able to work toward the building up of
the body of Christ by love. Not only is this an emblem of
steadfastness and strength in our walk, about our hips appears the
girdle of Truth, which is described by the word 'Jewels'. In
Ephesians 6 v14 we are commanded to put on the girdle of Truth.

We must understand the Gospel of Christ and the truth of the
cross and the resurrection of Jesus so that we are not swayed by
any false doctrine or fanaticism. Error will not hold us together or
keep our feet from slipping in dangerous passes. Only a girdle
woven by the hand of God, out of the truths of God, can hold us
together as we go into the valleys of humiliation and abasement
from others.

---

[32] Ephesians 4 v 14-16.

V.2: Your navel is a rounded goblet that never lacks
blended wine.
Your waist is a mound of wheat, encircled by lilies.

The body or the navel is compared to a goblet full to overflowing with red wine, and this figures the clasp that holds the girdle together. This ruby clasp holds the girdle together and keeps it immoveable. The ruby wine symbolizes the New Wine of the Kingdom. Only through the spilt blood of the Jesus Christ can the maid put on the girdle of truth which binds her firm in the faith, all held together by the red wine of the clasp.

The best wine reminds us of one of the first miracles performed by Jesus at the beginning of His ministry at the wedding in Cana. When the wine supplied by the steward ran out, Jesus filled to overflowing all the jars with His new wine, which was symbolic of His new life He was offering to all.

It is as we see ourselves crucified with Him upon the cross of Calvary, it is as we reckon ourselves dead to sin, to unrighteousness and to the flesh that the girdle of Truth is clasped around our waist. As the bride lives out the gospel day by day, she is enabled to walk in victory; and this full goblet that Christ prepared and filled for her is brought to others through her ministry.

Your waist is a mound of wheat encircled by lilies.

Jesus Christ is the only wheat in which there is no chaff; and the golden colour of the wheat is another emblem of Him. He is the

Love Divine

Bread of life, He is the only sustenance upon which believers can feed and thrive. The yellow wheat indicates the body of Christ, with all the food and nutriments, which come from Him alone. And around this are the lilies, which represent the followers of Jesus. We have in this Seventh chapter of the Song of Solomon a glimpse of the fruitfulness of the bride, the food and care which she brings to others and the love that she bestows upon them.

He sends us out so that we can feed others with the Bread of life and then they are planted in His garden, which is the Church. If God's perfect plan had been carried out there would be but one Church. Though there would be many assemblies, they all would have been of the same mind and preach the same Gospel. There would be no cold churches, no nominal church members, no churches walking hand and hand with the world and its pleasures, and many times with its sins. If we as the church wore the belt of Truth fastened together with the blood red clasp that holds it secure and unmoveable we would drink the New Wine of the Kingdom and be firm in our faith, recognising that it is through the spilt blood of Jesus that we are kept safe. But if we only gird our self with our daily goodness, or man's theories, we can only draw around our self man's efforts and strengths, which cause us to depend solely on human resolution. Then when we have our first attack of doubt, and maybe pain, we find that we cannot face obstacles. Then everything that binds us together shatters, and we find that any trust we had has left us, and we are defeated and very alone.

V.3: Your breasts are like two fawns, twins of a gazelle.

Here the daughters of Jerusalem see the beautiful breastplate of faith and love upon the bride. Without faith it is impossible to please God, for he that comes to God must believe that He is God and He is the one who rewards those that seek Him. As we love Him more, so our faith is perfected, for faith works by love. The difference between the first description of the bride's breastplate, and that which we are now considering, is that in Chapter Four it is the Beloved who is speaking of the life in His Beloved, but now it is the Daughters of Jerusalem, who are amazed at the maturity and love of the maiden. She was beautiful in His eyes before, but others now discern her beauty.

Before any on earth saw the love and faith that was growing in the life of the bride, the Lord commended her faith and love, and described her beauty with tenderness and love, but after His tenderness and descriptions of how He is beginning to see her, she had the experience of indolence and sleep. Now, those around her see her perfections and love for others. They see the love that is described in 1 Corinthians 13 vv 1-13 which is the perfect love and nature of Jesus Christ. They also see the faith in which nothing is impossible, the faith that can move mountains, the faith that continually looks to Jesus and His finished work. We need to keep our faith and love continually burnished through prayer, reading His Word, and living our lives according to His ways, so that the church of God will be powerful and inviting.

Love Divine

V.4: Your neck is like an ivory tower.

The neck of the bride has taken on the whiteness and stateliness of a tower of ivory. In Ch.4 v 4, the Beloved described the maid's neck as strong in Him and with the power of conquest. He has given us 'power over the enemy' and wants us to use it. As we have seen before, now she appears different to her Beloved, and to those about her. Before her Lord she is humble, dependent and walking softly. Before the enemy she is victorious and fearless. Before people she is stately, clothed with meditation and a quiet calm.

Your eyes are the pools of Heshbon, by the gate of Bath-Rabbim.

We are not told that her eyes are like waterfalls. We are not told that her eyes are like a river that is rushing seaward over rocks and large stones. We are not told that her eyes are like the ocean which is controlled by the moon, and sometimes lashed into fury by winds and storms, but they are like the pools of Heshbon; still, deep quiet with a stillness that comes from a peace with the Lord.

'Bath-Rabbim' means 'the daughter, or city, of a multitude.' These pools are at the gate of the 'city of a multitude' where the throngs of people hurry by and crowd into the city; but the water is unmoved and unruffled. The joys and sorrows, the hurry and rush, the ambitions, desires and distresses of the multitude have never moved these quiet pools. Men may come and men may go, generations may come and go but these pools remain the same.

204

The bride may be at the very gate of Bath-Rabbim, but there is tranquillity in her eyes and appearance that the world cannot give or take away. Running water cannot reflect the blue skies and the sun. It is the still pool that reflects the sun and sky in perfect beauty. We cannot look at the sun continuously, just as sinners cannot look at the Lord, but all can behold Him in the lives of His followers, and often many judge the Lord by what they see in His followers. It is not when we separate ourselves from humanity as a hermit, or isolate ourselves from mankind as a recluse, that our eyes become as pools of Heshbon. This holy rest and meditation are perfected when we are doing the will of God, and faithfully performing the duties that he has given us to do, whether in seclusion or in outward confusion and hurry. Where ever we are, no matter how busy and rushed amongst multitudes of people, this stillness and peace can be perfected, because it comes from a life hidden with God.

I remember many years ago a missionary from America had a vision of the whole of the U.K being covered in darkness, but all over the land there were pockets of bright lights, some giving a wonderful glow and many just small lights, but they were pictures of the houses and buildings where the Holy Spirit was working and leading His people. She prayed that all these lights would come together, and that there would be revival in the land. I do believe there is a hunger in the land for people to find the reality of God in their lives, both in the established Churches, but also in the many, many fellowships where families meet together regularly for worship, prayer and teaching with groups of people from all over

Love Divine

the world, and in every county and city in the land. These are the lights and life that we pray will cover the whole this country and the world.

V.4: Your nose (or 'face') is like the tower of Lebanon, looking towards Damascus.

In the eyes of her Beloved as she looks towards Him, He sees her humility and meekness as she follows Him. This is not meekness in the way the world values attitudes and life, but the meekness that Jesus Christ lived and taught us. He left His home in glory, and humbling Himself He became a man, facing all the temptations and pain that we experience on earth. He was on earth for 30 years, and the last three years he experienced popularity, scandal and bitter hatred. He experienced the deep, unfathomable agony of Gethsemane that led to the humility and onslaught of Calvary. That is the meekness of Jesus Christ. I have heard it explained, I believe by Albert Schweitzer, as the humility of Jesus:

Submitting to the dealings of God without rebellion,
And to man's injustices without retaliation.

That is not 'meekness' as someone without assurance, or who has no peace about his place in life, and no understanding about his place in life before his God. It is the meekness of a man who will bend his will before his Father God, and who tries with the grace of God to love his neighbour as himself.

The Beloved sees the maid like a strong mountain tower on the border mountain, Lebanon, which looks over to the enemy country, and the hostile and treacherous town of Damascus. There is a precious grace in the yielding and humility towards God but it is also combined with the boldness that is relentless and unyielding towards the enemy and powers of darkness.

There is another meaning of the word 'nose'. It means quick of scent, quick of discernment: able to discern not only good, but also those things that are wrong and not true. If you ask God for the gift of discernment, you must be able to discern yourself; for God cannot trust you to discern others if you cannot discern your own life and attitudes. We must endeavour to be so close to the Lord that we will discern the least uprising or temptation within our self

V.5: Your head crowns you like Mount Carmel.
Your hair is like royal tapestry;
The king is held captive by its tresses.

We are not told that her head is like Carmel, but the head *upon her* is like Carmel. There are two different precious meanings embraced in this verse, which are encouraging and edifying.

Carmel was famous for its fertility and its fruitfulness, and the name 'Carmel' means the 'mountain garden.' The mountain was crowned with evergreen trees and famous for its fields of corn. So often we can become so self centred and have such a low perspective of ourselves that we forget the words that Jesus spoke

Love Divine

to His disciples, and which Matthew reminds us at the end of his gospel Matthew 28 vv 18-20:

> *All authority in heaven and earth has been given to me.*
> *Therefore go and make disciples of all nations, baptizing*
> *them in the name of the Father and the Son and the Holy*
> *Spirit, and teaching them to obey everything I have*
> *commanded you. And surely I am with you always, to the*
> *very end of the age.*

As God's disciples on earth we forget that we need as Christians to speak to others and with the help and grace of God to bring them into the Kingdom.

Paul towards the end of his life tells us in his second letter to Timothy 4 vv 7-8:

> *I have fought the good fight, I have finished the good race,*
> *I have kept the good faith. Now there is in store for me the*
> *crown of righteousness, which the Lord the righteous*
> *Judge, will award to me on that day- and not only to me,*
> *but also to those who have longed for his appearing.*

This crown of righteousness referred to in the Song as the crowning glory of the evergreen trees and golden corn that crowns mount Carmel, is symbolic of the crown to which Paul is referring. The bride has not only the encouragement of the shepherds and teachers of other living souls, but the crown of righteousness

208

which is laid up for those who fight the good fight, who finish the course, who keep the faith to the end.

Even in the Old Testament the words of Isaiah tell us

I have placed you here on earth as a light for other nations:
You must take my saving power to everyone on earth.

This is not just an optional extra which we may desire to obey or ignore; it is part of God's plan and desire for everyone He has created on earth in His own image. If we are willing He will give us the grace to achieve His desire.

Your hair is like royal tapestry; the King is held captive by
its tresses.

This verse refers to the crown that Jesus wore and is mentioned in Hebrews 2 v 9. 'But we see Jesus, who was made a little lower that the angels. Now crowned with glory and honour because he suffered death, so that by the grace of God he might taste death for everyone.'

Paul also tells us in the book of Romans in which he reveals to us so much of the gospel of faith and our life in Him:

Now if we are children, then we are heirs of God, and co-
heirs with Jesus Christ, if we indeed share in His sufferings
In order that we may also share in His glory.

The royal tapestry is made up of red, blue and gold thread, representing red for suffering, blue for heavenly blessing and gold

Love Divine

for divinity and purity. It is as we partake in the sufferings of Christ, and we put on His heavenly attributes, that we will reign with Him. It is as we try to attain this life, to be one with Him so shall we reign with Him in his glory sharing His crown.

For those who follow the Lord all the way and don't count the cost, He grants in some small measure to drink of the cup that He drank. If we read of the great saints in the past, or of those today who suffer and are killed because of their faith and trust in Him, or who just live to love others: they partake of His sufferings and will also reign with Him in glory.

The Beloved still continues to praise and tell the maid of all the delights that He sees in her-

V.6: How beautiful you are and how pleasing, O love with your delights!
Your nature is that of a palm. And your breasts like clusters of fruit.

We all in our lives are driven to admire and praise others. Maybe it is because of their extraordinary achievements against almost impossible circumstances, or maybe simply because of their steadfastness against great adversity in what appears to others to be an ordinary life. This admiration may not always be because they have an underlying faith in God, but just because they recognise the faithfulness of others. Many who claim to have no belief in a living God but are intrigued and look and study different religions and faiths, all the time declaring that they don't believe in a God who created the world and all that is in it, but so often they always

210

seem to be searching for the truth. Also many who know and love the Lord are inspired and encouraged by the life they see lived by others, and the way those who believe and trust in Him face adversity and death.

What a delight and wonder it would be to hear these words from the Lord, but what a dangerous past-time it would be for us to even contemplate such words for our self.

Your stature is like a palm tree, your breasts like clusters of fruit.

Often as we try to describe the Lord just as the maid tries to describe her Beloved, or we speak of our love for Him it so often seems not possible or deep enough to use everyday words, and we resort to other means to declare our love. So it seems with her Beloved as He describes the beauty of her, not as the world see her, but He tells us all that He sees within her.

First, her growth and strength are described, then the fruit and faith of her love.

The palm tree always grows near springs of water, and often encourages a weary traveller to press forward and take advantage of its water and shade. As her stature is as a palm tree so He sees in her the comfort that even if standing alone she can bring to others, and give them the living water of life. When Christians come together and begin to chatter amongst themselves, it becomes a sharing of the water of life. There is also shade from the trees, and many who are feeling weak and worn with the cares of the day find comfort and encouragement. The palm is a stately tree that does

Love Divine

not lose its leaves, it always seems to be flourishing as its bushy branches grow taller and taller on the top of its stem as it grows higher and higher. It is an emblem of constancy and patience, of fruitfulness and victory.

It is also remarkable for its long life and the fruit from its top branches. So the Beloved is telling the bride that she is like a tree planted by hidden fountains of water from which she draws her life. She brings her fruit in season, and her leaves never wither, and as she draws her strength from the fountain of water, which is her life in Him, and so her roots spread out further. The long life of the tree symbolizes the eternal life that believers have in Jesus Christ. As the Bible tells us, 'God has given to us eternal life, and that life is in His Son. He that has His Son has eternal life.'

Only as the bride draws from Him who is the 'Fountain of living water' can she become strong and bear fruit as the palm tree.

V.8: I will climb the palm tree; I will take hold of its fruit.
May your breasts be like the clusters of the vine,
The fragrance of your breath like apples,
And your mouth like the best wine.

Those who have been watching the bride are drawn towards the Beloved whom they know has done such great things in her life. As she speaks to them of salvation, and the promises of God they see the fruit of these promises in her life. They begin to realise that salvation and heavenly blessings are for them too, that 'Whoever will come and drink of the water of life will receive this new life freely'.

212

They begin to realise all that God has done for any one of His children, He is willing to do for all who come and acknowledge him as the Son of God. The One who paid the price for the sins that separated them from the love of God the Father. They never again need to live without Him or walk alone.

When a hungry soul is brought into contact with those who are strong in the Lord, those who know Him in their lives, and have a hunger to bring others into the Kingdom of God, and who walk closely with Him, the hunger of others will be increased. It is the strong who encourage the faint hearted, exhorting them and reassuring them; praying with them and for them; until from being weak -hearted they come from the knowledge of believing in their head and knowing Him in their heart. When the strong give others the cluster from the vine, the New Wine of the Kingdom, those who receive it will have a new life far more abundantly than they ever will realise. All of this is imparted through faith working by love in those caring for the vineyard of the souls for whom Christ has died. It is not inconsistent that the bride of Christ should be spoken of as though she were the source of the food and drink which belong to the Kingdom of Christ. She is not the source but the channel; she is the body of Him who is the source of life and of all spiritual food and drink. She is His body; and it is through the members of His body here on earth, that He is working and doing even greater things than he did through His human body in which He walked on earth.

Love Divine
Jesus Christ the Son of God.
He is greater than any ruler,
Mightier than any warrior
Nobler than any king
Wiser than any sage,
Bigger than any kingdom
Better than any crown
Lovelier than any name
Worthy of all worship and deserving of all praise.

Roy Lessin

The fragrance of your breath is like apples, and your mouth
like best wine.

In the second chapter, the bride describes her Beloved to the apple tree among the trees in the forest. The more the bride feeds upon Christ, the more the fragrance of her Christ-life is seen in others. In the natural the breath bears the odour of what has been eaten. In the spiritual world if we are continually feeding upon the fruit of the incomparable Apple tree so the air around should give forth the fragrance of the Divine Apple. As the working of self and its activities leave us so we know the complete rest and peace that is in Jesus Christ. Sometimes when we meet together with others for prayer and meditation the presence of God is almost tangible, and not only does God meet with us then but also when we approach Him alone. As we ask and pray in the 'Name of Jesus', His love is poured upon the prayer and the breath of the one fruitful Tree our prayers go through to God and bring down answers to the glory of His name.

...and your mouth like the best wine.

This is how the Beloved speaks of the mouth of the maid and all that He hears from her. What would it mean for the glory of God if our words were like a running brook of living water, fed by springs, pure and sparkling? Words that are like streams, watering every place and giving life to everything they touch.

There is another thought here too, that all our words should be under the banner of God. He alone can bring us to a place where every word, even the common place that appear to have no connection with the Heavenly should be fit for our Beloved to hear. How many times when we are open to the Spirit of God He will give a gentle check to what we are about to say. If listen to these checks of the Spirit, no matter how peculiar it seems to those about us, we shall find that God will take more and more control of our words. In the place of idle unworthy words will come words of exhortation, of truth; words of instruction and encouragement. When we fail which so often does come about a silent prayer of attrition will help us to go forward once again.

In the third chapter of James we read, 'We all stumble in many ways. If anyone is not at fault in what he says, he is a perfect man, able to keep his whole body in check.' However a little later we read, 'Likewise the tongue is small part of the body, but it makes great boasts. Consider what great forest is set on fire by a small spark...it is restless evil, full of deadly poison...with the tongue we

215

praise God, and with it we curse men who have been made in God's likeness.' This should not be so- words spoken in the right place and at the right time are like apples of gold in a network of silver. Proverbs 16: 'A wise man's heart guides his mouth and his lips promote instruction... Pleasant words are a honeycomb, sweet to the soul and healing to the bones.'

How solemn is the thought that when we have spoken, the words can never be taken back, and their influence can go on and on. Even after we have died the effect from much we have spoken still abides whether for good or evil. Words that sometimes cripple others for the whole of their lives. When we speak ungracious words, whether to anyone or about any one we are taking our place among fools, as the proverb declares, 'The words of a wise man are gracious, but the lips of a fool will swallow up himself.'

What anguish some of us have had as God made us see the solemnity of our words and actions. How many times through hastiness and lack of wisdom, or through the working of our flesh, have we been rash with our mouths. How many of God's children colour the truth to wound one another; and those words may be forgiven, but when once heard, the scar and pain remains.

Maybe we need to continually ask the Lord to help us be more aware of the Holy Spirit in our lives, and to be more alert to His check on our words, so that all we say will come under the banner of His life.

It is generally assumed that the maid and the daughters of Jerusalem speak the next ten verses. Having seen the changes in her life and the peace and happiness that she has in her Beloved and His life, they have turned to Him and agreed to follow in His ways and His desires for their lives. It is a new song that has-been put in the mouths of the daughters of Jerusalem. So often it seems that no tongue can describe the joy and rejoicing that fills the soul that has really come to the Lord and tasted the fullness of His salvation; into whose heart and life the Lord has come to take full possession, coming right into our being so that he can work out His will in our life. Sometimes there may be a time when we do not want the Lord to be so close. We may know about Him but we want to live our lives according to our own desires and not trusting in His love. When young people on the threshold of their lives, make a commitment to the Lord, I am so impressed. For the first twenty years of my married life we went to church as a family, and I always believed in Jesus, but I still wanted to run my own life. When I first began my new life with Him, I felt so sorry that I had taken so long to bend my knee and missed so many years of my relationship with Him. As soon as we really accept Jesus Christ as our Saviour for whatever underlying reason our hearts rejoice and say, 'My beloved is mine and I am his.'

Our first joy is the consciousness that He is ours. We begin to know that He is ours in a real way, as though there was no one else to claim Him and His love, although we are aware that He is the Lord and Saviour of all believers. We rejoice that He is ours, and we draw on His protection and working on our behalf. This is our first joy, and then we find that as we go on with the Lord the relationship between us grows more intimate; our love is drawn out

217

Love Divine

because of Himself rather that because of what He does for us and our possession of Him and our hearts cry out -

Ch.6 v 3: I am my Beloved's and my Beloved is mine.

We have begun to see that we have given ourselves to the Lord to be His forever. That He has not only given Himself to us, but that He requires from us the understanding that we are no longer our own but that we have been bought with a price. Only this attitude can bring us under His desires so that His purpose can be carried out and His name glorified. It is when we have passed through hard things our responsibility towards Him breaks more fully upon our understanding and the fact that we *are* His, also begins to fill our spiritual consciousness in a deeper way. It is only when she has passed through times of spiritual desolation and calamities from the world that the maid has the peace and knowledge of Him to be able to say –

V.10: I belong to my Beloved, and His desire is for me.

There are three wonderful and awe inspiring ways of our communion and growth with our life with the Lord.

First we rejoice that He is ours, secondly then as we draw nearer there is a deep joy and rest in the consciousness that we are His in life and death, and we ask for His will to be accomplished in our life, although we may still be longing for the approval of the world. Finally, our consuming satisfaction is that we are not only His, but His desire is towards us. Though we know from the first that we are His, but we feel that we have not entered fully into His life. It is when we realise something of the cost, and we are able to say 'Not my will, but your will Lord, no matter what you ask of me,' does our relationship really begin to change. In the beginning we have rejoiced that He is ours, we have known He is ours, but we have not taken upon ourselves or been willing to enter into His will and His ways whatever the cost.

> *V.11: Come my Beloved let us go to the countryside, let us*
> *spend the night in the villages.*
> *Let us go early to the vineyards*
> *to see if the vines have budded,*
> *if their blossoms have opened,*
> *and if the pomegranates are in bloom.*
> *There I will give you my love.*

The gardens and vineyards are synonymous, meaning the Kingdom of God. We see that at this time there is the bud and the flower, the newly ripened fruit and also the preserved fruit. Everything is found in this garden except the spices.

In the first chapter of Acts, Christ tells His followers that they shall be His followers, that they shall be His witnesses, both in Jerusalem, and in all Judea and Samaria, and to the ends of all the earth. One meaning of the word 'witnesses 'is, 'martyrs'. There is significance here which shows it is not over an easy and smooth path that the Spirit-filled and Spirit-called servant of God walks as he preaches the gospel of Jesus Christ. It is with suffering and persecution, that God's faithful servants proclaim the gospel. The

Love Divine

servant of the Lord and the gospel he is preaching and teaching to bring new life into the world, needs to have The Lord with him all the way.

The maid first takes the Lord into her mother's house, she wants her family to meet Him and follow Him. She then proclaims Him in Jerusalem and wherever she goes, and as her soul draws closer to her Beloved her heart goes out for the Kingdom of God and she cries 'Come my Beloved, let us go out to the ends of the earth.' She does not say 'let me go forth' but 'let *us* go forth,' even as her desire is to travel further and work harder, uppermost in the truly consecrated mind of her soul is the communion she will have with Him as they work together. Through personal work and prayer, through supporting the work of God where ever she is she becomes like the prophet Daniel in Ch.12 v 3 who says 'Those who are wise, will shine like the brightness of the stars in the heavens, and those who lead many to righteousness, like the stars for ever and ever.' There is a deep love expressed in this passage for those who are ignorant of the love of the Lord, but there is also the precious reminder for all of us as Christian people we must continually feast on the word of God and live it until it is manifested in our own life, before God can use us to lead others into a deeper experience and knowledge of Him.

Years ago when I had a career that I loved, the Lord clearly said that I should let it go. With the encouragement of my husband I perhaps slightly grudgingly did just that. I then felt that I was just left to look after the family and clean the house. One morning after cleaning the bedrooms I complained bitterly to the Lord that I had left a fulfilling job with many responsibilities. In fact I had often thanked Him that I was so fortunate to have such an enjoyable job. Immediately He clearly said, 'Read my Word', so I stopped and opened my Bible and turned to Galatians 1 v 15-18, (I thought by accident!). These verses tell us that when God called Paul to bring the gospel to the Gentiles, even though he was one of the most learned of the Jews, he went into Arabia to seek God and learn the truth he was to preach. He tells us that even after 14 years, he met again with Peter and the other apostles to discuss the question of circumcision.

I realised why I had left my work: I now had more time to read and study, and go to the Bible study classes during the week. I began to read the book of Romans with a commentary, which also began a deeper walk with Him. I was to prepare myself to be available should God lead me that way.

The maid asks her Lord to go with her to see if there is any fruit on the vine or flowers in her vineyard, is she saying to Him,

Search me O God, and know my heart;
 try me and know my thoughts.
And see if there be any wicked way in me,
and lead me in your way everlasting.[33]

These were the words that David replied to God after God had explained to him that He knew about His troubles, He knew everything about him even before he was born, he knew what

---

[33] Psalm 139.

Love Divine

would happen in his life, and there was nowhere in the whole world where he could he move away from Him.

V.13: The mandrakes send out their fragrance, and at our door is every delicacy both new and old,
That I have stored up for you my Beloved.

The mandrakes are known as love apples, and are also said to increase the fruitfulness of those who eat them. It is when the bride has let the Lord go into every part of her life, not keeping certain areas or thoughts away from Him, and entrusting herself entirely to His wishes and direction, she gives Him all of her love and adoration which is symbolized by the continual fragrance of the mandrake. It is not the works of the flesh that are fragrant, but the fruit of pure divine love. When she has let the Lord mould and make her into His disciple that the fruits and vines begin to flourish in her vineyard, bearing fruit for His glory. He can trust her to go out into the vineyard of the world as a co-worker with Him in the lives of others. It is then that her love flows more fervently for others, and as she partakes of His love, so her fruitfulness is increased and multiplied for His glory. When the Lord does healing restoring work within us, (and sometimes we are ignorant of the fact that we need it), He does it gently and thoroughly so we become a more whole person, and able to accomplish anything He may ask us to do. How can we speak forgiveness to others if there are areas of unforgiveness in our own lives? No wonder we need to continually be on our knees!

Spirit of the living God, fall afresh on me.
Melt me mould me fill me, fall afresh on me.

John Ch. 21 is one of my favourite stories in the Bible, (and I have mentioned it before) but in it we see how Jesus lovingly restores Peter's relationship with Himself. The Bible tells as that Peter was able to speak to the crowds after Pentecost, explaining what God was doing amongst His people, and he told them, 'This man Jesus of Nazareth whom you killed is alive today, healing with mighty works and wonders, you crucified and killed Him by the hands of worthless men.'

If we want a close loving working relationship with the Lord, we must lay everything about us bare, and let Him enter into every part of our lives.

Love Divine

CHAPTER EIGHT

V.1: If only you were to me like a brother, who was nursed at my mother's breast!
Then, if I found you outside I would kiss you, and no one would despise me.

When we long and desire for a closer touch and clearer revelation of the Lord, such as the disciples enjoyed when He was on the earth, speaking with Him face to face, and long for the veil that hides Him from our eyes to be lifted, that we may cry as the bride and say, 'If only you were my brother, part of my family, and I had the right to kiss you.'

Maybe the maid is longing for a kiss of affection from such as a brother. A kiss of acceptance from someone in her own family, perhaps intimating that they still had an affection for her, and did not despise her for her love for her Lord.

Historically, this is after the Lord's ascension, and is speaking to us of the fervent love and desires and stress of those left behind. Those who knew Him and had spent much of their lives with Him longed for His return and the renewal of the personal contact and companionship that they enjoyed with Him before His death. The disciples must have had the sweetest and most intimate companionship with Him while He was here on earth; they had lived with him day by day, remonstrating with him, and even questioning Him when they could not understand His words. This special, wonderful intimate relationship was never the same after

His death. When Jesus was on the earth He was a man just as they were except He was also the Son of God, but they always met on the same common ground. After He came from the tomb His body was a spiritual human body; but they could not meet in exactly the same way that they had known before. They would not have that same relationship with Him until they, too, should lay aside their mortal body and put on their spiritual body in heaven. He walked, and talked and ate with them, just as they had known Him before, but then He would just disappear from them. It must have seemed to them there was now a particular majesty in Him. Sometimes today we may find this puzzling. Some say that Jesus is a Spirit, and that since His resurrection there is nothing about Him that shows His humanity, others go too far in recognizing His humanity, but seem to forget that He is the Son of God. If we look to the Word of God it tells us that the word 'Resurrection' always signifies the raising of the body from the tomb, and does not apply to a person's spirit, which goes to God who gave it to us as soon as it leaves the body. It was not the Spirit of Jesus Christ but His body that was raised from the dead. Even the marks of the nails and the spear remained, even though His body had become different to the one He had on earth.

When Jesus rose up into heaven it was not a spirit that ascended, but it was the same Jesus who had appeared to the disciples, who had eaten with them and talked to them since His resurrection. As the disciples listened and talked to Jesus they saw His wounds which proved to them it was their beloved crucified Lord, and when they suddenly saw Him taken up to heaven it was the same resurrected body that they knew, not a Spirit. Two angels or messengers of God in white clothes spoke to them 'O you men of Galilee, why do you stand looking into heaven, this Jesus, who is received from you into heaven, shall come back in the same manner as you see Him now.'

Timothy in his first letter, chapter 2 v 5 says 'For there is one God, and one mediator between God and men, a man Jesus Christ who gave Himself a ransom for all.'

We are not told that He *was* a mediator or that he *was* a man, but that He *is* a mediator, and *is* a man. Whatever changes took place in His body, from the time He died to the time He ascended to the Father, we know that it was a human body that came out of the tomb, and yet it was a spiritual body without the limitations that it had before His death. That was the body that ascended into heaven and took His place at the right hand of God, and which was again clothed in His glory and was seen by Paul and others. During His time on earth after his resurrection He looked the same as when He was on earth except for the signs of the stigmata. When Thomas doubted the words of the disciples that the Lord was alive on earth again, Jesus did allow him to touch the wound in His side to prove whom He was, but He also seemed to wrap Himself in such majesty that He filled His disciples with awe and reverence. When they wanted a closer intimacy, or constrained Him to be to them as He was before His death he vanished out of their midst.

Sometimes God's children today who love Him and look forward to the time when they will be with Him forever, and have the close intimacy with Him which will be as much above the relationship that the disciples had with Him on earth, as Heaven is higher than the earth. Then our body will be conformed to the body of His glory through grace of His power and love. Then there will be no limitations or weaknesses that will mar our relationship with the Lord. Though now we find comfort and peace with Him during times of prayer and meditation, we still sometimes long for the comfort of His right arm about us, and His left arm to show us the way. Sometimes circumstances happen so that we feel our only comfort is to be physically held by the Lord. When this longing is great, for comfort, I turn my thoughts to remember again that I know He knows everything about me, even my thoughts, and that there have been times when He has stepped into a situation without me physically asking in prayer and a situation has been saved from a calamity. This may read as a comparatively unimportant situation, but had not God provided a trained chef I would have been up most of the night quite a long way from home when a small team of us were preparing the food for a wedding reception for two missionaries in our church, three hundred guests were expected at the marriage supper the next day. I was standing in the kitchen with twelve turkeys waiting to be carved, the ham had been sliced which seemed comparatively easy, but I was facing these most difficult looking turkeys I thought I had ever seen. Suddenly a voice said 'I thought you might need some help' and behind me stood a professional cook, whom I did not know well, but she kindly listened to the prompting from the Lord, even though it was quite late in the evening, and offered her help. In no time the birds were expertly carved, complete with all the sinews drawn from the legs. I knew that if this had been left to me, without the fine expert carving she was able to do, the meat would not have looked so appetizing to be presented to the guests, and others and I would have had very little sleep.

V.2: I would lead you and bring you to my mother's house-she who has taught me.
I would give you spiced wine to drink, the nectar of my pomegranates.

In this verse the bride is explaining to her Beloved that she wants to take Him to her home, so that others may know the joy that is hers, and also that they may be drawn towards Him, and as they hear and listen to His voice they might seek Him themselves. When we meet others of God's children who have not accepted His love, and seem to be struggling in life on their own quite unaware of the love and life that they are missing our hearts feel sad and we yearn for them to come into the Kingdom. Only Jesus Christ can instruct us and guide us along the way we should go. Sometimes we may be attracted to the wonder of a beautiful sunset, or the wonder of a newborn child, or the kindness of a stranger, which causes us to ponder and think more deeply and overawes our minds. Such moments in our life are as though God draws open a brake in the clouds to let a brilliant sun shine to reveal Himself to us. We may be drawn through a sad tragedy, or the sudden death of one we love, but God is always waiting for us to turn to Him. We may have to go down a bitter path of changing hurt and rejection into love and forgiveness towards others before

Love Divine

we will grasp His hand. If we consider the love that Mary Magdalene had for Jesus, and her continual quiet presence amongst the disciples as she followed him and listened to everything He taught, she loved Him so much because she was one who had been forgiven much and so loved with all her heart.

In Walter Wangerin's book, *The Book of God* he so excellently interprets the whole Bible to read as a novel. The Financial Times said that Wangerin's aim 'was to produce a clean, continuous story free from repetitions and genealogies, and to add in bits of cultural and historical background based on his own travels and scholarship. In all of this he succeeds.' As Jesus travelled He often had the twelve disciples with him, and certain men and women whom He had healed, and many women, particularly Mary from Magdala. Mary, described as poor, pale and bruised, ministered to Jesus quietly serving His personal needs of food, cleanliness, clothes, rest and music. She never drew attention to herself. She had no family in Magdala. This was her family. If she could not be a daughter, she could be a servant. If she could not be a mother then she could be a maid. It was enough. But it was also so that she experienced a very precious, caring closeness to the Lord. She had received a new life and, always wanted to be with him. Wangerin tells us that she of all seemed to know something of the trouble in the soul of the Man of God, and was aware that He may be taken from them. Mary Magdalene remained small and thin and hushed. She would not draw attention to herself, she would not jeopardise the delicate gift that had been given to her. Walter Wangerin then tells a story of Jesus on the Sabbath speaking and teaching in the synagogue in Capernaum, and Mary was sitting among the women listening, and I quote 'she often turned her eyes toward the cloak that Jesus was wearing, and the blue fringes on it. She had washed it the night before, using a new mixture: a gentler alkali and liquid dripped through the ashes of another kind of soapwort. The fabric of Jesus' garment was delicate. It had begun to wear thin from too many harsh washings. She meant to try to preserve it- but not at the expense of cleanliness.' An absolutely charming story obviously well researched, but also amusing, I am sure we all are guilty of our wandering minds even when listening to the most brilliant of speakers, perhaps even of the Lord.

In verse 7 the maid tells us she is longing to give to her Beloved spiced wine to drink and nectar from her pomegranates. During the Last Supper that Jesus had with the disciples before He was crucified the next day, He commanded us to eat the bread and wine in memory of Him, and He solemnly declared that He would not drink the fruit of the vine with them again until they were in His Father's Kingdom. Matthew 26 v 29. It is for the marriage supper in Heaven that the bride is longing to drink with Him in His Father's Kingdom. There is every fragrance and spice in this wine; it is full of all the attributes of Himself that He has given her, together with all his spices that she will drink with Him in the Kingdom. She will give Him the nectar of the sweet juice of her pomegranate. The 'pomegranate' here is used as a symbol of the bride's humility given by her Beloved, and is the apparel of a meek and quiet spirit. The word 'Juice' comes from a root, which means,

Love Divine

'to trample, squeeze, to bruise'. This describes the process of extracting the juice from the fruit prepared to make the wine. The value and life of most fruit is in the juice; and when that is extracted the pulp that is left is not edible. There is also a deep spiritual meaning here too and that is the description of the process through which the precious vintage of inward humility which is brought forth within us. It is through many hard things, through much bruising and bringing down that this costly wine of humility is made and perfected within us by the Lord. Sometimes it is by the pressure and bruising from those about us, and different things that confront us daily working together with the purifying pressure of God's hand upon us that brings about in us the pure nectar of humility as symbolized by the juice of the pomegranate. Just as it requires great quantities of fruit to make wine from the pomegranate, and after the fibre and hard seeds have been removed, and the flesh pressed out to make the juice that symbolises the pure humility within us. It is not mixed with fleshly humility, or pride because of the work of the Spirit upon us. Those in whom God is working and perfecting this precious fruit are unconscious of what He is doing; we may only be conscious of the instruments He is using and the need for contrition and meekness within us. It does not come from voluntary humility, and penance and self-effort striving to be humble.

Vv.3,4: His left arm is under my head, and His right arm embraces me.

Daughters of Jerusalem, I charge you: do not arouse or wake up love until it so desires.

This entreaty to the daughters of Jerusalem occurs three times in this book; but this relationship with the bride and her Beloved is only experienced once in Ch. 2 v 6. In this passage we are now considering, the bride is not experiencing his right hand as she did when He took her into His Banqueting House. She is longing for a closer touch, and to again enter into a deeper experience with the Lord, such as the joy mixed with deep reverence when we reach the gates of Heaven. Very often when we make our first commitment to Jesus, to give us encouragement He will give us a special boost in our young new relationship, which woos us into a greater abandonment. We may realise that we know Him better than ever before, we know that He has worked deeply within us, and we are not the same as we used to be, but inwardly we long for a deep spiritual experience. As we mature we realise that we may not again receive the same experiences and revelations that the maid came to know in the Banqueting House with him Ch. 2 vv 4-7. However when we look back we realise again that He has never been far from us and His hand is never lifted. As we grow and meditate upon Him, and we know that He is the same today and forever, it does not seem so important to have especial times of encouragement. Because we know deep in our hearts we can always trust Him and we want Him to know that we can be trusted.

Love Divine

V.5: Who is this coming up from the desert, leaning on her Beloved?

As we read and study this wonderful book we must keep reminding ourselves whether we are reading it considering the relationship between the maid and her Beloved or are considering the relationship between the Lord and the body of Christ on earth, or are we considering our own relationship with Lord.

Historically this verse is referring to the early Church and the first fruits of the Lord's ministry on earth.

What wonder and amazement must have seized those who first saw and experienced the miracles of the early Apostolic Church in the first days of its power, beginning with the outpouring of the Holy Spirit upon believers. This commenced on the day of Pentecost; and afterwards the many manifestations of the mighty workings of God that followed. All who saw the three thousand added to the church in one day must have called 'Who is this coming in from the desert leaning upon her Beloved?' The same question must have been voiced when Jesus came back from the wilderness full of the Holy Spirit and power after having been tempted by Satan, and also was the same question asked of the early church and the apostles as the people believed in Him and followed the Lord. The apostles themselves questioned Paul when three years after his conversion he came back from Arabia to be amongst them. They were amazed how much Paul had learnt, having received such a depth of knowledge from the Lord so that he might bear His name, he also received his commission to take the word of God 'before the Gentiles and kings and the children of

234

Israel.' Paul lived the rest of his life living and teaching the gospel of Christ, in spite of his many imprisonments, beatings, shipwrecks and suffering. Still today we are indebted to his letters and teachings written to the different churches he had planted to encourage the people not to renege on their faith in Jesus Christ. Paul listed the dangers he had encountered in a letter to the Corinthians, 2 Cor, 11v 23-33. Not to boast, but to encourage the people to turn back to God, instead of taking up again their lives of sin, 'not repenting of their impurity, sexual sin and debauchery in which they have indulged.'

The bride recalls the time soon after she came to know the Lord for herself, after her first joy she began to be enticed by sleep and had become indolent in wanting to progress in her new life. But here we find her purified and restored; her spiritual beauty increased and her gaze fixed firmly on her Saviour, as she yields more fully to the leading by His hand, and lets Him lead her wherever He wills. Nothing matters to her except His will; she wants to know Him to be supporting her according to His every direction.

As St. Paul said, 'I can do all things in Him, to be content in any and every situation as He strengthens me.' Paul's life completely submitted to His Lord enabled God to bring life to thousands as he travelled through Egypt, Judea, Syria, Galatia, Macedonia and Rome. Today his writings and letters are still the motivation for many students young or old.

Each one of us needs to come individually up from the wilderness to the Lord, but Christians from all over the world are

Love Divine

finding more and more that the whole world is a wilderness. There is more persecution and hatred practised in the name of God than ever before in this 21st. Century, and we all in whatever situation we live in must keep close to Him in prayer. We are not all asked to lay down our life for Him, but when we are overcome by pain and tragedy, by rejection and wrong doings we need to trust in the strength of His right arm, perhaps let some parts of our lives which we trusted and hoped would be of some service to the Lord go, and let every situation come under the anointing of the Lord. Paul said:

I have been crucified with Christ and I know longer live but Christ lives within me.
The life I live in the body, I live by faith in the Son of God, who loved me and gave His life up for me.

He was a true man of God who also was obedient unto death.

The Beloved again addresses the maid and encourages her with His love.

V.5: Under the apple tree I roused you; there your mother conceived you.
There she who was in labour gave you birth.

It is always through the drawing of God that we find salvation, He will draw us, but He will never make our knees bow. The maid found her salvation in Ch. 2 v 3 as she sought Christ in the trees of the wood, she found Him under the shadow of the Apple Tree. Among all the trees of forest of men, she found life when Jesus

236

found her. As the sinner comes to Christ and so to the foot of the cross he begins to take the fruit of the Tree and receives life everlasting. It is when Christ hung upon the tree that He became the one fruitful Tree. He tasted death for every man and was made perfect through sufferings in order that He might lead many to Glory. It was under the shadow of His cross that we were found and born again. It is there He found us, and it is there that we find Him; the man who is our hiding place from the wind, and the covert from the tempest. It was there, that streams of living water flowed out towards us, and from that Rock the streams still flow even more abundantly. This precious Rock, always with us as we press on in our heavenly journey

V.6: Place me like a seal over your heart,
like a seal on your arm;
For love is as strong as death,
its jealousy unyielding as the grave.
It burns like blazing fire, like a mighty flame.

The bride is with her the Beloved, and now there is a deep fellowship that binds them together, which does not depend on conscious presence or absence. She knows that a time of separation is coming, maybe a prolonged absence is evident and her desire is to cling to Him, to the love that gives her life, her cry is to her Beloved, to remind Him of her dependence upon Him. She wants Him to bear her seal upon His heart and on His arm. He is going to His Father's house where He will prepare a place for her, and she

Love Divine

implores Him not to forget her, but to uphold her by His arm and to hold her in His heart as he stands before God on her behalf.

In the Jewish Tabernacle, the high priest always bore the names of the tribes of Israel upon his shoulders and upon his breastplate. The shoulders or arms are symbolic of strength, and the breastplate is symbolic of the heart and affections. This was a symbol of our High Priest, 'who bears us upon His heart and upholds us by His strength as He stands before God; for Christ has entered into heaven itself, now to appear before the face of God for us.'

It is as our Beloved is continually in our hearts, as our love goes out to Him, and we lean upon Him in all things, that we apprehend and enter into the rest and sweetness that we are engraved upon His heart. It is as we look into Him that we receive and enjoy his love and faithfulness, which surrounds us continually. He wants us to so trust in him that we should never be dismayed, knowing that whatever comes before us He is with us. He wants our communion between us never to be broken, and for us to know that we are set as a seal upon His heart. The bride having come through all her trials and difficulties knows that her Beloved has promised to set her as a seal upon His heart.

Revelations 3 v 12 tells us exactly what was written in the Song of Solomon centuries before when St. John came face to face with God on the Isle of Patmos.

Him who overcomes I will make a pillar in the temple of my God. Never again will he leave it.

I will write on him the name of my God and the name of my
city of God, the New Jerusalem...
And I will also write on him my new name.

V.7: Many waters cannot quench love;
Rivers cannot wash it away.
If one were to give all the wealth of his house for love
It would be utterly scorned.

This passage is often used to describe human love and jealousy. While human jealousy is utterly scorned and is aligned with covetousness, the meaning expressed here is altogether different. I have read that the literal translation of this passage is, 'For love is mighty as death; jealousy is as exacting, or relentless as hell.'

There is much that is comforting and reassuring in the little word 'for', which introduces this description of divine love and jealousy. The bride has been imploring the Beloved to set her as a seal upon His heart and His arm. She knows that if she is sealed upon His heart, His love, which is as strong as death, will forever hold her and uphold her. Nothing can extract her from this place of privilege, and with jealousy as exacting and unyielding as Sheol, He will fight for His own possessions and protect His own seal. He will not let any evil or harm come upon her. We are told in Deut. 4 v 24 ' Jehovah is a devouring fire, a jealous God.' We see this also in Exodus 34 v 14.

'Jehovah, whose name is Jealous, is a jealous God.' He gives all, and He demands all. The love of God is stronger than death.

Love Divine

'Neither death, nor life, nor angels, nor principalities, nor things present, nor things to come, nor powers, nor height, nor depth, nor any other creature shall be able to separate us from the love of God, which is in Christ Jesus.[34]

When we experience the power and strong grasp that death can hold on a loved one, and nothing can bring them back from this silent relentless grasp, so it is with the love of God for His children; and so it should be for our love for Him.

It is this divine love, which is given to us, deep in our hearts through the Holy Spirit that has brought the bride to a place where she can forsake all others and release all ties that demand anything of her that is not the right of the Lord alone. When we read the Holy Scriptures we begin to see the holy zeal, which is the working of a holy love towards God. When Jeremiah was fearful of even using the name of God, because of his reverence towards Jehovah, he felt that there was such a' burning fire' in his bones, because of his holy zeal and fear of God, that he opened his mouth and spoke the words of God to the people. Because of his obedience his life became a span of persecutions and dungeons and opposition from the people. He was one of the many, such as Moses, Elijah, Samuel and others in the Old Testament and millions more in the last two thousand years who have paid the price for us all. All whose love and zeal was such that they counted their life as nothing, compared to the joy of doing His will. Some we hear and read about, but many others only the Lord knows who they are, and know the suffering and cost that many have endured,

---

[34] Romans 8 v 38.

and still do today. He knows those who love Him with all their heart, all their mind and all their strength, and love and serve their neighbour more than themselves. As He promised He will prepare a place in heaven for each one of them.

Many waters cannot quench love;
rivers cannot wash it away.

In the Scriptures the word 'water' is often used as a figure of God's wrath and in situations of His displeasure and anger; also for trials and afflictions. The word 'floods' is used as a figure of extreme dangers, also of violent assaults by the evil one.

When we remember and read of the violent suffering and invectiveness that the Lord passed through, we see that many waters cannot quench love, neither can floods drown it. As He hung on the Cross at Calvary, all the waves and billows and darkness of God's wrath went over His head. All the floods of the devil and his hosts came up against Him as He wrought out the redemptive work which God had given Him to do. But nothing quenched His love for His Father or for the world. The prophetic words of the 22nd Psalm give us a faint glimmer of the suffering of Jesus, as in verse 20:

Deliver my soul from the sword,
my life from the power of the dog! (Satan.)
I will tell of your name to my brothers
In the midst of the congregation I will praise you.

Love Divine

In this verse in Psalm 22 Jesus is praying, 'I pray not for the world, but for those you have given me. I pray not that you should not take them from the world, but that you should keep them from the evil one, or as expressed in the 22nd psalm 'Deliver them from the power of the dog.' Again we hear the Lord in John 17 vv 20-23: 'I pray not only for those who know me, but for those who believe in me through the written word... that they may be as one, even as we are one; I in them, and you in me, that they might be perfected into one.' It is as He poured out His life that He bore us through the waves and billows of God's wrath, and planted us on the firm Rock of Himself.

V.7: If one were to give all the wealth of his house for love it would be utterly scorned.

These words written by Paul in 1 Corinthians 13 explain the life of Jesus:

Though we speak with the eloquence of angels, and the tongues of archangels without love we become sounding brass and a clanging symbol. Though we prophesy and know all mysteries and all knowledge, though mountains remove and vanish before our faith we are nothing. Though we give our substance in small portions, so that it may reach many, or give our body to be burned, and have not love, it profits nothing.

242

Many may be pouring out all good works, and giving their lives for others but if they have neither love for God or for man they are trying to work their way into Heaven. They may look upon God as a hard taskmaster, and fear that He may be watching for some delinquency in their lives. They do not realise that when our love for the Lord is deep and strong we are more concerned for Him to work in us, and to change us for His glory, that maybe we are to work for Him.

Though we may give God our time our money, our facilities, and deprive ourselves of all but bare necessities of life in order to give to Him and His work, but have not learned to give Him the first place in our hearts and lives we have nothing. We will have no peace that surpasses everything, and there will always be part of us that is never fulfilled.

God has made us to know Him. He wants us to give our love and ourselves back to Him.

V.8: We have a young sister, and her breasts are not yet grow...
What shall we do for our sister, for the day she is spoken for?

Historically, this refers to the concern and perplexity of the early church concerning the Gentiles being brought in to the Kingdom, after there was undeniable proof that they were included in God's plan. In Ezekiel 16 v 46 the Gentiles are called, 'The sister of the Jew'. The Gentiles, as yet, have heard the gospel in only spattering instances; and the Jewish believers, seeing that God

Love Divine

has visited the Gentiles too, are perplexed to know how to bring the gospel to themselves. The Jewish ceremonial laws, and the question of circumcision concerned the whole church. It was through the Holy Spirit that God revealed to the early church the mystery of the gospel: 'that the Gentiles are fellow heirs, and fellow members of the body, and fellow partakers of the promise in Christ Jesus through the gospel.'[35]

Then the question was asked, what should we do with our little sister in the day she is asked for? Only through hearing the Word comes faith and love, and many of the Gentiles had not yet heard that. They had not put on the breastplate of faith and love; their breasts (their love and faith) were unformed, they were not ready for either marriage or bearing children for God, because of their deep prejudice, which the law of Jehovah had fostered in them. It is only the Jewish people who can know the perplexity this caused in the early church.

The Jewish people were forbidden by the law that God gave them through Moses, to have any dealings with the Gentiles, the Jews all were circumcised and became proselytes. When they were faced with the revelation that the Gentiles were fellow heirs and fellow-members of the body, and also fellow partakers in the promises of Christ Jesus, the very foundation of their religious worship seemed to drop from beneath their feet. They would have required the Gentiles to enter the church of Christ through the door of circumcision, and become approved through diligently keeping the law. Through these differences came much contention and the

---

[35] Ephesians 3 v 6.

244

question was asked: 'What shall we do with this little sister, now that we see she is spoken for?'

V.9: If she is a wall, we will build towers of silver upon her.
If she is a door, we will enclose her with panels of cedar.

The wall and door are the two principal parts of a building. The wall is a symbol of strength and in Isaiah 26 v 1 where the psalmist is singing a song of praise we read, 'We have a strong city; God makes salvation its walls and ramparts.'

Here we are told that we shall have a strong city, and Jehovah will appoint Salvation for walls and bulwarks. In this verse in the Song of Solomon the Jewish believers are saying that if the Gentiles prove to be a wall, they will build upon her a turret of silver. As we have said before, 'silver' is a symbol of atonement through which God brought salvation to the world. Comparing the verse in Isaiah with the verse we are now considering, we see that the walls are to be a figure of Salvation; and Salvation came only through the atonement of Jesus Christ. The converted Hebrews determine that if the Gentiles receive the Gospel and turn away from idols and turn to the living God thus becoming strong in the faith, they will not push upon them the Jewish rites and ceremonies. Peter discussing this matter with the early church in Acts 15, is quoted speaking the words of Jesus:

If you obey my commands, you will remain in my love, just
as I have obeyed my Father's commands and stayed in His

Love Divine

love. I have told you this so that my joy may be in you and that your joy may be complete.

In other words there must be no dead works built upon the wall of Salvation. 'Therefore let no man pass judgement on you in questions of food and drink, or with regard to a festival or new moon or a Sabbath. These are only a shadow of what is to come; but the substance belongs to Christ.'[36] The wall of Salvation was to be built through simple faith in Jesus Christ, and in the atonement He wrought on the cross on Calvary.

This little sister, the first Gentile coming into faith must be a strong wall but also a door, which is the only entrance into the building. 'God opened a door of faith for the Gentiles'.[37] Christ is the door for the sheep, but there is a beautiful reference here, that the little sister must be enclosed with boards of cedar, which is a symbol of Christ's sinless manhood.

V.10: I am a wall, and my breasts are like towers. Thus I have come to His eyes like one bringing contentment.

This new church grew so rapidly that in a short time she was a wall, and her faith and love were like the strong turrets of the wall. It is through faith we put on Jesus Christ, it is through faith the boards of cedar enclose us, as we are enclosed in Him. Paul relishes in the faith and love of this new church of converts. Paul speaks of the faith and love of the Colossians towards the saints,

---

[36] Colossians 2 vv 16-17.
[37] Acts 14 v 27.

246

and he rejoices in the work of faith and labour of love of the Thessalonians. As we read of the faith and love shown by the early church, recorded in the New Testament, which tells us that the Gentile church was as a wall, crowned with the beauty of the finished work of the atonement of Jesus Christ.

V.11: Solomon had a vineyard in Baal-Hamon;
he let out his vineyard to tenants.
Each was to bring for its fruits a thousand shekels of silver.

'Baal-Harmon' literally means 'The owner of a multitude.' Not only is Jesus Christ the owner of a multitude, He has planted His vineyard in the midst of a multitude; and the multitude are planted in His vineyard. In the Old Testament we are told that the people of God were as the sands of the sea, and throughout the book of Revelation, we see that the Redeemed are pictured as a great multitude, which no man can number. Under the Law, the Vineyard of the Lord was conditionally given to the Jews; and this is represented in both the Old and the new Testaments as a vineyard that is let out to keepers. A scripture that vividly portrays the unfaithfulness of the Jewish nation and the transference of the Vineyard of the Lord to the Gentile Church, is told in a parable in Matt. 21 vv 33-44: The householder built a vineyard and surrounded it with a hedge; he let it out to managers and left for a far country. The treatment of the servants who were sent to receive the profits of the vineyard was always harsh: some were beaten, some were killed by the managers. Finally the merchant sent his son and heir who was also killed.

Love Divine

To many this parable perfectly shows the way the Jews persecuted and killed the prophets of God, and finally they killed the heir, Jesus Christ. At the end of the parable we are told 'The Kingdom of God, shall be taken away from you, and given to a nation that will bring fruit to the world.'

In this portion of the Song the maid is speaking, she is of both Jewish and Greek blood, of both bond and free. The vineyard has been taken away from Jewish nation of the unfaithful keepers, and given to the Gentile church. The bride now most earnestly makes a covenant that she will be faithful to give to Solomon the thousand pieces of silver, which is his due, and to those who keep the fruit shall be given two hundred pieces. In the book of the Song of Solomon, the keepers were to give a thousand pieces of silver to Solomon for the fruits of the vineyard, and the silence that follows this statement shows that they were not faithful in giving him his proper payment. This is brought out in the passage in Matthew and in Jewish history.

V.12: But my own vineyard is mine to give .The thousand shekels are for you O Solomon,
And two hundred are for those who tend its fruit.

Though the Lord may let us tend a portion of His great Vineyard, and let us minister to other souls in different ways, there is a part of the Vineyard of the Lord, which He actually gives to each one of us; and that is the vineyard of our lives. In this way He gives His Vineyard to His bride, each one of us receiving a portion.

248

The Lord wants us to guard our hearts above all that we treasure and protect, for out of hearts come all the issues of life. It is this hidden place that must be watched and tended more than all that appears on the outside. We cannot judge the condition within us by what is seen on the outside, because many times the outward appearance may be better than what appears before the face of God. When prosperity surrounds us, when everything seems to be going well in leaps and bounds we must be more watchful and diligent. It is when the way is easy, when the sun is shining as though no cloud should ever again cover it that self-confidence creeps in; the blight of carelessness and indolence strikes the vines of all that we do. When the enemy seems to have forgotten us, it is an indication that we must arm ourselves with more prayer and keep our shield of faith in readiness. All of us when working in the Lord's vineyard will experience times when the force of the waves and darkness and affliction will surround us in an attack to devastate all that we are doing, and the tempests and cyclones seem overwhelming, but it is then that we must turn to Him, and we will be aware that God can turn everything to good for those who trust Him and love Him. Psalm 73 v 25 says, 'Whom have I in heaven but you? And earth has nothing I desire but you.'

V.13: You who dwell in the gardens with friends in attendance, let me hear your voice.

It is a wonderful thing to live and work in the gardens of the Lord, this is where the waters flow and the Hidden Manna falls, and the Kingdom of God begins to increase. The greatest blessing

Love Divine

for those in the garden is that they grow closer to the Lord, and learn more of Him. The closer you draw to God, the more the Holy Spirit will lead and guide you; and as you walk in the Spirit so you will discern more quickly those words or actions, in your thoughts and motives, on your appearance and ways that are not the ways of Christ. This discernment will not come from introspection, from examining yourself, nor from wounded pride because of being discerned by others. It will come from a continual gaze fixed upon the Lord; a continual looking and listening to Him.

Let me hear your voice.

The Lord draws us to Himself; His desire is for us to live our lives with Him in every way. It is also imperative for us to stop and listen to Him.

V.14: Come away, my love, and be like a gazelle,
or like a young stag on the spice laden mountains.

Again for the last time the maid speaks to her Beloved who is unseen but near. The book opens with the cry from the ancient church for their Messiah. It also speaks of the hunger for those who make up the bride of Christ on earth; for all those who have a desire, and a clearer revelation of the Lord, and a greater entrance into His chambers and presence. We have been led over the pathway that the maid has trodden as she has obeyed and followed her Lord. At the end we find her diligently keeping the garden of

250

her own soul, while she works in the Lord's great Vineyard, but all the time watching for His return.

The Mountains of Spices are the fourth mountains mentioned in the Song of Solomon. Though the Mountains of Spices are closely connected, and in some ways identified with the Hill of Frankincense and the Mountains of Myrrh (the Tomb) they are used as symbols of the life of Christ. The Mountains of Spices arise majestic and eternal from the Cross and the Tomb, and are a symbol of the majestic eternal work fully accomplished by Jesus Christ. The Mountains of Spices symbolize His perfected finished work, through which we are redeemed and delivered from the hands of all our enemies; and through which we are able to accomplish our calling from God. Only through the Gospel does Christ come to us. When we approach the Mountains of Spices and believe and put His finished work on Calvary to the test as we yield to the cross in our lives, Jesus Christ reveals Himself to us in the Gospel. He is like a roe or young stag as He comes to us over the Mountains of Spices. It is over these Mountains (Christ's finished work on Calvary) that God and His Son come to us; and it is over these fragrant Mountains that we must pass to have access to God. As He reveals Himself to us, He shows us the power there is in the gospel, the 'Glad Tidings' of Christ's redemptive work.

We have followed the footsteps of the bride as we have studied this book, and the Holy Spirit has revealed to us how she has hastened to her Beloved when she hears His voice calling her. We have seen her hidden in the clefts of the Rock of Ages and seen her climb up into the vineyards of the Lord. We have seen her as

Love Divine

she travelled through the wilderness in the Chariot of Salvation, and maybe astounded by the continual love and encouragement as the Beloved speaks to her of His delight in her, as she is willing to open her eyes to the shallowness of the world, compared to her life with Him. As we read and meditate upon these experiences of the bride, the Holy Spirit will open up the preciousness and understanding of the way He has led her. He will lead us to examine our own lives to see how far we have followed Him. When we desire to follow Him, He will re order our lives and all concerning us, He will open up His word to us until we are caught up in the chariots of His life. It may not always be easy to yield to Him and let Him take away our strength; but as we do this, He will manifest His strength, which is made perfect in our weakness. The harder and more that we will lean on our Beloved, the more we will enter into the precious experience of beginning to understand and know the Peace of the Lord, which no one can take away.

> *Jesus coming down from Heaven, come to me,*
> *Jesus born in a stable, be born in me.*
> *Jesus accepting the shepherds, accept me.*
> *Jesus receiving the Magi, receive me.*
> *Jesus dwelling in Nazareth, dwell in me.*
> *Jesus abiding with Mary, abide with me...*
> *Jesus the light of the world, enlighten me.* [38]

AMEN.   Come Lord Jesus soon.

---

[38] David Adam, *Border Lands*, SPCK, London 1991.

252

EPILOGUE

One of the reasons I felt drawn to write about this book in the centre of the Bible, the Song of Songs, is because through many years of studying it I have learnt so much about the persistent, caring love of the Lord, and have been so encouraged in my own life through just these eight chapters.

Many people find it difficult to believe in a personal love between God and themselves. We may believe that Jesus is the Son of God, and maybe are beginning to understand why He died on the cross as the Saviour of mankind, but also cannot believe that God can know each one of us personally. Perhaps we may feel too insignificant, or we may feel unworthy and not good enough for God to be interested in us alone. Maybe we have gone to church for many years because it is the right way to behave, but no one has really explained that we can have a personal relationship with the Lord God. Perhaps the reason Jesus died on the cross has been explained, but we have never really 'heard' what was being said. To gain this relationship, we need to have the faith to believe that Jesus Christ *is* the Son of God; that He died on the cross bearing all the guilt and wrongs in our lives that have denied God and lived our life to please our self. Our attitude to life may be that we cannot be bothered with God or other people. We say 'I'm my own boss; it's my life; I can do what I like with it'- not aware that this is sin, the 'me first' attitude, which, like a thick cloud that blocks out the sun, will block the way to God in this life, and in the life to come. The consequence of this attitude is that God will feel miles away. A Holy God will not and cannot not look upon sin. He hates sin, whatever we have done. Our saving grace is that He is also a God of love, and He has proved that love by giving his only Son to pay the price for our sin by dying a horrific death, taking upon Himself the price that we should pay for all our sins, so that we can have a sinless relationship with His Father, if we believe in him now we can have a personal relationship with Him on earth and throughout all eternity.

God's character is like a coin with two sides: justice and love. His justice rightly condemns all sin, and will cause a barrier between us and a Holy God, which must be punished; His love makes Him long for mankind to become his friend again. On the cross, God's justice and His love were perfectly satisfied. God's perfect sinless Son was the only one who was good enough, (without sin) to pay the price for us.

One of the most famous verses in the Bible is in the Gospel of John 3 v 16:

God so loved the world that he gave his only Son, that whoever believes in him should not perish but have eternal life.

Have you ever taken this step? Maybe you have felt that your life is not very satisfactory, you have given philanthropically to those in need, you have often offered to carry a bag for an elderly person, you try not to steal or take anything that is not yours, but there still seems to be something missing. You have tried to satisfy yourself by using your money to buy expensive holidays or 'toys', or entered into lots of relationships that still have not satisfied you, and you are beginning to think that the whole of your life feels meaningless. In each of us there is part of us that only Jesus can satisfy. The book of Genesis tells us that we are all made in the image of God; we all can be creative or artistic, a searching scientist or a compassionate social worker. There is something of God that is in each one of us. No other creature on earth has the ability to worship someone or something. As someone said there is a 'Jesus sized hole in our heart' that no one but He can satisfy.

Maybe you have never realised that there is anything for you to do. You can be baptised, confirmed, go to church, even read your Bible and pray, and still leave Jesus Christ outside the door of your life. We all need to face this question honestly and ask Him to come into our life by His Spirit. Is Christ outside your life or inside?

Will you let Him in or keep Him out?

You cannot ignore Christ's invitation forever; we never know what we will have to face in the future.

King George VI speaking to the nation in his Christmas talk during the Second World War quoted this message to all of us:

> *I said to the man who stood at the gate of the year, 'Give*
> *me a light that I may tread safely into the unknown'. And he*
> *replied, 'Go out into the darkness and put your hand into*
> *the hand of God. That shall be better than light and safer*
> *than any known way.'*

Here is a simple prayer to pray if you want to put this situation right:

Love Divine

'Lord Jesus Christ,

I know I have sinned in my thoughts words and actions,

There are so many good things that I have not done,

There are so many sinful things that I have done.

I am sorry for my sins and turn from everything

I know to be wrong.

You gave your life upon the cross for me.

Gratefully I give my life back to you.

I ask you to come into my life.

Come in as my Saviour to cleanse me.

Come in as my Lord to help me.

Come in as my friend to be with me,

And I will serve you all the remaining years of my life

With the grace and help of the Holy Spirit.'

If you have prayed this prayer – however hesitantly – but meant it, what you have said is a fact. You have asked Jesus Christ to come into your life and He has come. He now lives in your heart by His Holy Spirit.

Don't rely on your feelings, you may not feel any different at the moment. Trust His sure promises. You have begun the journey into your life with Him and you are now at the start of a new life. You have in Christ Jesus an all powerful, ever present Friend who is always with you.

Very often the book of Acts in the New Testament is said to be the book about the work of the Holy Spirit working directly in

256

our lives, which it is, but again some say that those miracles were only for the early church 2000 years ago, and are not relevant for today. However many people worldwide can testify to the fact that God is real, and is as active now, just as in the first century. He wants to be relevant in every part of our lives, not just in our Christian activities.

Having looked into this fascinating book, The Song of Solomon, I want to explain how God worked in the lives of our family and those surrounding us when we began to prepare for the opening of a shop and small restaurant in the city of York, called The Mustard Seed. Through it I hope you will see how God was real at this particular time, leading and guiding us.

Several years ago in York our family, (that is my husband and myself, and our three children, even if they were not all actually living with us at this time) and with the full backing of our church were embarking on a new ministry. We envisaged opening a shop or meeting place selling gifts and books, morning coffee and possibly light lunches. Our aim was to create a peaceful, special place, which was available to the public, and was also somewhere Christians from different churches, and people from different countries could meet and chat together. We hoped it would be a small beacon of God's Kingdom on earth. We also hoped it would be used by some of the hundreds of tourists from all over the world who throughout the year visited the ancient city of York, many especially coming to the beautiful Gothic Minster which was on the opposite side of the road from the premises which we were hoping to rent. At that time a super market and another business were bidding to acquire the fairly large shop, but we prayed and believed that if the desire was right according to God's will, somehow we would be accepted by the agents.

We knew this would entail selling our house in the country to raise the capital to restore the shop, plus the three floors above to provide a home for our family, all of which would of course mean putting our furniture in storage until the premises were ready. At that time we had no idea that after we had found the right property it would take nearly nine months before all the floors were made habitable, and we would be ready to open the doors of the shop.

Both of our sons had already left home, but fortunately our daughter had decided after she had finished her training as a nurse that she would like to be available for any need in the church. We also had two young women living with us both of whom shared the vision of the shop, and wanted to be committed to the work.

Very fortunately for us, our family was invited to live in the church house, which was home for the curate and two other single people. This arrangement meant that my husband and I, our daughter and two young women who also were with us, plus our beautiful Labrador dog and marmalade cat were to live together in this quite small house. Eventually, admittedly feeling quite nervous and apprehensive for the future, we walked up the narrow pathway to the front door; I remember thinking that most probably those who were on the inside of the house would also be feeling very nervous and apprehensive! As the curate welcomed us all in, and we filed past him through the front door, he said, 'I am reminded of the verse in Hebrews, 'Here am I, and the children God has given me.' Those few words did the trick and we all relaxed and laughed, but we did not realise how long we would be in this situation. The writer of Hebrews used this verse from Isaiah 8 v 18:

Behold, I and the children whom the Lord has
given me are signs and portents in Israel from
the Lord of hosts, who dwells on Mount Zion.

Isaiah was trying to console himself against the wicked ways of the children of Israel. The prophet was speaking to the God of Israel, complaining about the people's wicked ways. God told the prophet He was still in control, in spite of their disobedience. He would forgive them because they were His children. He had taken them out of captivity, and they were now travelling towards the Promised Land, they were a symbol of God's control in all situations,

I was encouraged by this word and I began to realise that even if we had many difficulties ahead, and even if they were of our own making, the Lord would not abandon us. I also remembered the fact that the two young women with us had come to us without our seeking them, and were also a sign that God was with us in the whole of the situation.

Our aim was to create a shop or business that was to be part of God's kingdom on earth, just as there are many such places all over the world. Somewhere we could meet people, be able to speak of our faith naturally and easily, and to witness and speak of a loving living God who wants to be involved with the whole of our lives, if we will let Him.

We had been praying for such a place for two years, and I was wandering how we could ever manage to get this project together, even though several people were willing to give up their careers to be part of it. Also attractive articles and gifts had already been given to us to sell, but how would we ever be able to speak about our faith and to encourage others? Most probably customers would just come in for a brief respite from shopping or their feet ached from the old uneven paving stones in many of the streets in York. Maybe they just wanted a cup of tea.

Apart from getting everything off the ground, how would conversations begin? We didn't want posters or banners because they could 'spiritualise' us, or cause alarm in others.

I had been in business as the under manager of a large store in York, but then we had accountants, and stock control experts, and even buyers for some of the stock.

Also we still felt that we needed many more people to be involved, and I was not yet sure what we should we sell, or whether we should consider serving more than just tea, coffee and biscuits.

I knew we could serve and sell to people good food and have attractive things in the shop, after all there were many such places in the city of York. I had watched many customers being beautifully and thoughtfully catered for in other restaurants. Often they would enter chattering and talking, enjoy their meal, pay the bill and leave still chattering and talking, just enjoying their day.

We could not intrude on their conversation, nor had we any right to talk about our faith when the customer only wanted a particular book, or a good lunch.

I also realised that if we were endeavouring to live our lives according to God's ways, and through His grace seeking the righteousness of Jesus and sharing our lives together it would not be easy. I especially was concerned for those who had come to join the team and had already given up a big part of their lives for the vision, either by putting their careers on hold, or leaving their own living accommodation. I had to learn that the problem was not mine to solve, all I had to do was continually pray and then leave everything with Jesus.

We eventually had a team of about twelve young people, some coming from far away, and also local folk in York, plus our very supporting Church fellowship. Some of the team lived with us, others were invited to live in the rectory with the Reverend David Watson and his family, and many in the fellowship opened their homes, providing a family and support for others who needed a base. We all would need to keep close to our heavenly Father, and learn to rely on His wisdom and guidance. This meant that not only would we work together, and pray together, but also learn to love and respect each other as brothers and sisters in Christ.

Not only did we pray for the staff that we needed, and what we should sell (we needed to cover quite a formidable rent), we prayed for how much stock we would need to run a viable business to cover rent, rates and staff wages. We also prayed for the practicalities of our lives living and working together.

Love Divine

Incredibly very soon wonderful situations began to evolve. Just two examples of God working with us was the fact that when we realised that we were to serve lunches as well as teas and coffee, and so we would need a commercial kitchen. A young woman, who had already come to live with us had been the head of the Domestic Science department, in a large school in London. She understood about the preparation for large quantities of food, and how to present it professionally and safely. We also had living with us an Oxford scholar with a degree in theology and philosophy, he also knew and understood all the needs of installing a commercial kitchen, because for a brief period he had worked in a London restaurant. We soon became well known for his super bread and his particular selections of coffee. One young man came to see us who could neither read properly nor calculate any money, having had a very difficult childhood; he also wanted to be part of the team. However his faith was very genuine and he had a great love for the Lord. He learnt all the skills he needed by the patient teaching from one of the church's youth workers, at the end of his busy day with us. It was so encouraging when this young man would share a verse or part of the Bible during a time of prayer, having learnt to read and to feel sufficiently confident with us. He eventually began to serve customers, and always was a willing hand in the kitchen, preparing most of the vegetables for soup, salads and curries; he had a great gift for serving and encouraging others. We were not surprised when his mother came to love the Lord through his ministry. In spite of practically no education at all, he was a good gentle soul, a servant for God.

The financial reward of only a few pounds a week which was suggested by the staff meant that we were able to have extra money to help support a missionary in Taiwan and also enabled us to release money for any need in the world or the U.K. The extra bonus for us all was that through the difficulties and hard practical work, our own faith was strengthened. We learnt to trust God for all our needs, and to understand more of His especial love.

A young woman on the team was planning to get married, and needed a wedding dress and I felt time was running out a few weeks before her wedding. Her parents were still in Australia so my husband offered to give her the money for her dress. She had come to the reality of her faith soon after she came to England under the ministry of David Watson in an evangelistic service in York Minster. She had always been part of the team right from the very beginning, and now needed a wedding dress; but only had enough money for a return fare home to Australia in case she needed to leave in a hurry. She did not want to take any money from us, but said she was praying. Maybe because I was worried that we would not be ready in time I offered to help her make one, and asked her if she had a special design in her mind. 'I would like it to be in special stiff white silk, with a long train at the back, and to have a soft cowl over my head trimmed with swansdown, with swansdown trimming on the neck and sleeves. I knew that I could never achieve such a dress, but she held onto the verse 'I know all the desires of your heart,' from Psalm 20 v 4. Still the wedding day was getting closer. Then one day, a young woman whom we hardly knew, had sent for her wedding dress, which was still in

Australia to see if it was the sort of dress Joan wanted. When the parcel was opened the wedding dress in it was exactly in the style she had been praying for, and perfect for a winter wedding. He is a caring God.

We also wanted to know what we should sell, and how much stock to hold. Again, I knew when I was in business in a large store we had accountants to help make that decision. I knew I could buy commercially if I needed to, but we always wanted to involve people who would bring us well-made interesting articles, and bring us unusual things to sell. We began to realise that we should have a small restaurant, serving coffee and lunches, with simple good food such as homemade bread and soups, various salads, apple pie and homemade cakes. We prayed that the Lord would bring to us those He wanted to be part of this ministry. I had engaged staff in my previous work, and made mistakes, but at the time had never thought of bringing these needs to God in prayer.

This time I wanted God to bring to us those people He knew who wanted to walk more closely with Him and would fit in with the vision that we had shared. We also considered selling music from our own church, greeting cards and Christian books and works of art.

An example of the Lord answering prayer was when three ladies came to see us, offering to make children's clothes for us. Their enjoyment was to spend time together, and sew; we had the pleasure of being able to sell beautiful children's clothes at a reasonable price. Two of the ladies began to be very interested in our faith as Christians. Another experience was from a group of people living on the other side of the Pennines in Lancashire; they had formed a group to make children's toys to give employment for those who were unable to get work. Unfortunately the toys they first brought were not of a sufficient standard to sell, but their ideas were good. We suggested that they should come back again, and the next time the toys and ideas were excellent, they gradually built up quite a sizeable business, and surprisingly we were able to export some of their work to Greece.

When I realised that all the preparations seemed to be moving forward very quickly, I wanted to know how the business would 'work.' We could prepare everything so that the whole of the premises would be honouring to God, good, clean and wholesome, but we needed something extra for customers to openly talk to us. While I was away with Philip at a conference, one of the speakers used the verse in Matthew 6 v 33, 'Seek first the Kingdom of God, and His righteousness, and everything will be added to you.'

Like a clarion call from heaven I knew that verse was an answer to my prayer. No matter how well we managed everything with courtesy and care, the most important aim was to seek God's Kingdom. Then through the work of His Holy Spirit our desires would be fulfilled. In other words if our aim was to live in His kingdom, and before everything else we desired, to follow the guidelines of Jesus, God would help us to achieve our desires according to His will. This was quite easy to say without thinking. I realised that it would mean opening our lives to the Spirit of God within us, and He would accomplish some polishing and maybe some cutting of His stones to bring His righteousness in our lives.

Love Divine

If we think of a diamond when it is found is quite dull and possibly ragged, but when it has been cut and polished it is a thing of beauty. In our lives working and living together we needed the Spirit of God to work deep within us, and his Spirit would show us the way.

> *Holy Spirit, come, confirm us*
> *In the truth that Christ makes known;*
> *We have faith and understanding*
> *Through your light alone*
>
> *Holy Spirit, come console us*
> *Come as advocate to plead,*
> *Loving Spirit from the Father,*
> *Grant in Christ the help we need.*
>
> *Holy Spirit, come, renew us,*
> *Come yourself to make us live.*
> *Holy through your loving presence,*
> *Holy through the gifts you have.*
> *Holy Spirit, come, possess us,*
> *You the love three in One,*
> *Holy Spirit, come of the Father*
> *Holy Spirit of the Son.*
>
> *Brian Foley b. 1919.*

We had a small card on each table telling how the idea of the shop had come about, and also explaining that we all were part of

266

St Michael le Belfry Church, which was situated a hundred yards from us, nestled alongside York Minster. We invited visitors to the services, and explained the availability of the staff in the church (or any one of us) should they have any questions or need any help or advice.

I often wondered how so many people from abroad knew about us. One day when there was a long queue for a table for lunch, I began to chat to some of those waiting, hoping that there soon would be a table available. A man in one group told me that a friend from Virginia had sent him our card to Los Angeles in California, suggesting that if they came to the U.K. they should come to see us. Then the family just behind them said 'We have come further, a friend in New Zealand sent us your card, and we have come from Tasmania.'

We often had the joy of ministering to customers, and encouraging others in their faith. Philip my husband was not directly involved in the work, but he was a wonderful encourager, especially when we needed words of wisdom. Before the shop opened every day, we prayed for the vision of the work, and practical needs for the day, and also for the grace to be open and caring for each customer. At the end of the day we again prayed for God's hand to be upon those we had talked to and served and then began the big clear up and preparations for the next day.

What were the consequences of this venture?

I still believe that through the viability of the shop it was very easy to talk about our faith, or answer questions quite naturally with others. Many people enquired about what motivated us.

Love Divine

Some people are shy and wary of evangelistic talks, so we often organised an especial dinner for those we knew, and those who were regular customers. We usually asked an evangelist to speak after the dinner, perhaps someone well known, whose name would encourage some of the public to come and be with us.

So began the Mustard Seed, which just grew and grew.

When I meet and talk with those who were so much a part of our life then, I always find that there is a deep bond between us, and so often we have remarked that it was one of the richest times in our life, but also proved to be very busy, and very demanding. So often when a problem arose, if we stubbornly refused to act in the way that we knew was of God and wanted our own way, then frictions had to be restored. We soon learnt that God's Holy Spirit will help us to achieve our aims, and if we open our lives to Him, so He will continue to work deep within us for His life to grow in our hearts.

Recently I came across an embroidered sampler, on which these words had been carefully sewn by perhaps a young girl in the 19th Century,

Life is not remembered by the things that take our breath-but the moments that take our breath away.

Those words so describe our life in the Mustard Seed.

Two years before we opened, while we were still living in the church house, the Lord used the Song of Solomon to encourage me. I had been feeling frustrated and overwrought about the position we were all in. One Sunday afternoon I went upstairs to spend a time with the Lord. We had sold our house, our furniture was in store and many of the people who were living with us in these cramped conditions had given up their cars, put university on hold or had to leave their home. There were three other people living in the house and three girls had a small room with just two beds; they would take it in turns to sleep on the floor. What if I had made a mistake? While I was praying I felt that the Lord wanted me to turn to the Song of Solomon Ch.2 v 10-14. I began to read these verses:

Arise, my love, my fair one,
And come away.
O my dove in the cleft of the rock,
In the covert of the cliff
Let me see your face,
Let me hear your voice.
For your voice is sweet,
And your face is comely.
Catch us the foxes
The little foxes
That spoil our vineyards,
For our vineyards are in blossom.

I prayed and meditated upon these verses, amazed that they seemed so personal.

When I eventually returned downstairs a visitor had arrived, she had stayed with us for a week or so, several years ago but had not kept in touch. She told us that she had been working in a

Love Divine

kibbutz in Israel, and was on her way home to America to arrange her wedding. She was breaking her journey for a short stay in England, and asked the Lord whom she should visit in the U.K. He gave her my name, and somehow she had found where we were temporarily living in York. After a brief chat and catching up on news she told me the verses that the Lord had put into her mind; they were from the Song of Solomon Ch.2 v 14-17.

I have no doubt who is the author of the book. At that time I was not very familiar with The Song of Solomon, but I was comforted by the words and text that this young woman shared with me. It was also wonderful therefore to rest in the situation knowing that the Lord was aware of the problems that we all were experiencing. I began to realise again that in any difficulty we were to love and trust Him, and react with positive thoughts and His grace. The 'little foxes' at the end of the verses refer to wrong attitudes or experiences in our lives, but I took comfort from the words 'because our vineyards are in blossom'. They were very encouraging, I took the picture of the vines in blossom, that even now before the premises were ready our new work had begun, and that even in this difficult time the fruit was not far away.

So began my many years of studying The Song of Solomon, and also so began the shop called The Mustard Seed. The whole experience was one of the most incredible times in our life. We found many people wanted us to talk about, or asked us specifically about our faith, and many asked for help in their own spiritual life. I still believe that to meet people from every background or need this was a good practical way of serving others, and creating a venue for those who may not be part of a Church, but had a belief in Jesus. As they entered the Kingdom of God, so His Spirit would be free to minister to them.

A few years later Philip and I were invited to be part of a ministry team in India, and while we were in Mumbai we met the nurses and nuns in the Mother Theresa Centre. The nuns were looking after babies and children in vast sheds, another huge shed for men in need, and even more accommodation for women. In many cases the patients were terminally ill. In spite of the simplicity of the wards without any of the sophisticated equipment that we expect to see in developed countries, there was a great sense of peace and calm. The nurses must all have had tremendously busy lives.

We had left the chaotic city, with crowds of people everywhere, often living in horrific conditions, amidst the constant roar of seemingly lawless traffic. Sometimes there were whole families cooking and sleeping on the central reservations on the frantically busy roads. As we walked into the quiet peaceful reservation, a few young boys were kicking a football around and one little boy as soon as he saw Philip immediately jumped into his arms. Everywhere we were met with a tremendous sense of peace, and the presence of a loving God. I remembered too that all these nurses were women who had given up everything to be 'handmaids for the Lord.' Their whole lives were undergirded with prayer, and we were invited to join them in a simple room, just as any of us might meet in our own home, and as we had done every morning

Love Divine

and evening in the Mustard Seed. I would not try to equate the work we did in York with the self giving of these wonderful nurses, but I saw in their faces the 'light, and peace' that others told me they had seen in the men and women working in the Mustard Seed. We were never aware of such in our own lives, we were just busy, but like these nurses, they all had at this time laid down their careers, given up their own living accommodation and way of life and had begun to trust the Lord for all their needs.

This testimony is just a short example of living a life with God. We happened to be involved with Christian work, but there are many, many more thousands of people throughout the world who can testify in their own daily lives to a living personal God.

ENDS